for Jean Blum

**4**

## content

## credits

**photography** John Back (pp 7, 9, 15, 55-57, 61, 64);
Ben Blackwell (pp 67, 68/69); David Heinlin (pp 63);
Fernando van Teylingen (pp 24, 25, 26, 28, 30/31);
Philip Ritterman (pp 49, 50/51); Leo van der Kleij
(pp 40-43); Dennis Adams (pp 65); Florence Paradeis
(pp 16, 17, 18, 19); Roos Aldershof (pp 34-37); Jouke
Kleerebezem (pp 78-79); all other photos Andrea Blum
**typography** Jouke Kleerebezem
**scans/typesetting** Set Service Amsterdam
**print** De Briefhoofden Amsterdam
**first edition** 600
**publisher** Stroom the Hague Center for Visual Arts,
Spui 193-195, 2511 BN Den Haag

**financial support** by the Mondriaan Stichting,
PBK ('Office for the Realisation of Public Projects') Dept.,
Amsterdam; TU Twente, Enschede; De Paviljoens, Almere

**isbn** 90-73799-24-4

**many thanks to** Lily van Ginneken, Jan Wijle, Tom van
Gestel, Jan van Grunsven, Lia Gieling, Marian van
Tilborg, Hannah de Vries, Peter J. op den Brouw, Jackie
Ferrara, Mondriaan Stichting

In 1992 realiseerde de in New York wonende en werkende kunstenares Andrea Blum in het kader van De Campagne van Stroom hcbk het werk *Surveillance Station(s)*. Met *Public Affairs*, dat zij in 1995 ook voor Stroom uitvoerde, het in 1996 aan de TU Twente opgeleverde *Information Plaza* en de installatie *Polder* (De Paviljoens, Almere 1997) werd haar werk in Nederland nader geïntroduceerd. In deze uitgave wordt het gepresenteerd in de context van projecten die sinds 1985 tot stand kwamen. Public Affairs werd de verzameltitel voor het werk in de openbare ruimte, Domestic Arrangement omvat een serie sculpturale en architectonische werken voor binnenruimten.

In 1992 American artist Andrea Blum, commissioned by Stroom, the Hague Center for Visual Arts, realized a series of works entitled *Surveillance Station(s)*. With the 1995 *Public Affairs* exhibition design, also commissioned by Stroom, and *Information Plaza*, that was presented to the TU Twente Technical University in 1996, and the 1997 *Polder* installation at De Paviljoens in Almere, her work was further introduced in the Netherlands. This publication presents these key works in the context of the development of a body of work since 1985. Public Affairs is the collective noun for the public works, Domestic Arrangement consists of gallery installations in Paris, Amsterdam and New York.

'The habits of domestic life are transposed onto the street. How we walk, talk, eat, relax is negotiated onto the scale of the public site. We leave our home and carry it like a backpack throughout the day. We take it with us out to the street, the theatre, the subway, the mall. We take our walls, chairs, libraries and vanities with us. We put on a coat and think of it as a warm bath. We buy a newspaper to fit around us like a mobile home. We sit in the park and find the same seat as yesterday. We drink a coffee to make the public space our living room. We take a train and get under the covers of the book. We wear sunglasses to separate our room from another. We look in car windows to try to locate our reflection in a context. We cross the street and try to remember why we left home.'

**6**

## Common, Place, Information

### the common

'...home is represen-
ted, not by a house,
but by a practice, or
by a set of practices.
Everyone has his
own. These practices,
chosen and not impo-
sed, offer in their
repetition, transient
as they may be in
themselves, more per-
manence, more shel-
ter than any lodging.
Home is no longer a
dwelling but the
untold story of a life
being lived. At its
most brutal, home is
no more than one's
name...'

John Berger
*And our faces, my
heart, brief as photos*

Common knowledge intensely differs from place to place,
it shines in local colors. Immediate experience is similar-
ly site-specific. On the basis of experiencee of characteris-
tic places we create maps to guide our intuition by chan-
ce of encounter and rules of traffic. Conventional media-
tion, mass media representation, infects the idiosyncracies of Everyman the Map Maker, but still even 'global'
information from sources outside our near environment
are accessed from and filtered by the intimacy of a body
in unique conditions. Maps violate this intimacy of mind
and body, to some even destroy it, drug our experience,
but even the 'cyborgs' can't voluntary dispose of their
prime reflexes or will they readily give up in-engineered
consciousness.

Maps are not the territory, but to a large extent (and
with information media data abundancy increasing) they
actively shape it. We learn to accept them as blueprints
to our perception and our motor systems. If we 'go' by the
book, we 'direct' by the map. Maps provide us with patterns and detailed information on the situations that we
find ourselves in. More so, they rule our perception of
them. Our map based mobility follows the traces of map
making rather than of any physical reclaim. Both their
hidden legends and more obvious imprints light-hearted-
ly play with motor nerves and muscles that place our one
foot in front of the other, that pull a smile on our face,
pop up goose pimples, or guide our hands probing skin
and resistance of the material realities that environments are made of.

Navigation hence is learning by experience, matching,
mapping. We ourselves inform our maps carefully by
moving about, by implementing and repeating 'sets of
practices'. These updates by the walks of life are mindful-
ly embedded as a reference to (be utilized when entering)
uncharted terrain, new places, different commons. The
information that we use to cross the street, to cross any
elongated space between two rows of houses, whether a
mud track or four lanes of asphalt—this guiding 'crossing
information' was gathered over time in ever so many
transits: our own, our family's, our neighbours', our
friends' and the many many street crossings mapped out
in popular media.

## Conversation between Andrea Blum and Jouke Kleerebezem

**JK** A lot of contemporary public art appears to have left the monumental, to foster a human scale, human practice. The monument demands attention, even humbleness—not participation. Monuments can be authoritarian
and are mostly supportive of dominant ideology. Monuments claim space and do not offer a 'stage' for negotia-
tion of information, memory, the social, the cultural, interaction, the sexual. Your public work maintains however a monumental, architectural scale, without being oppressive.

**AB** I am interested in the space in-between the monuments, the space reserved for arrival and departure, escape and refuge—sidewalk, doorway, catwalk, waiting area—appendages which are supportive of architecture, yet
remain invisible within the architectural hierarchy. My pieces are not presented as monuments, in fact they are

1994, Untitled (Leg)
(interior)

Materials: Masonite, Plywood,
Felt, Hardware
Dimensions: 152x125x125cm

An object is designed to function
as a chair while assuming the
scale of a small room.
The occupant is hidden from
view except for an opening which
exposes the upper leg for public
viewing.
The chair is blanketed in a grey
fabric which encircles the object
and frames the opening.

< I am interested in the space in-between the monuments

**8**

'...the house we were born in has engraved within us the hierarchy of the various functions of inhabiting. We are the diagram of the functions of inhabiting that particular house, and all the other houses are but variations on a fundamental theme. The word habit is too worn a word to express this passionate liaison of our bodies, which do not forget, with an unforgettable house.'

Gaston Bachelard
*The Poetics of Space*

Beyond our memories, according to Gaston Bachelard spaces are 'physically inscribed in us', as 'groups of organic habits'. In *The Poetics of Space* for example, he reflects the memory of our childhood house.

Without inscriptions like these we lack information and revert to commonplace. Commonplace, or default, reflects the acceptation of a status quo in which no information is updated, a *stasis* of no or strictly automated mobility. Commonplace defects imagination and makes its maps obsolete. The qualities that Bachelard attributes to the 'particular' house of childhood apply to other places, to other commons that left behind physical inscriptions of our mobility thus embedding knowledge of our environments. The informed map is imaginative, intelligent, sensuous, material and graphical, memorized and alerted when engaged in new conditions. Mapping memory, coloured by immediate experience and mediated information, is a complex reference system, a library not very well indexed but taken as absolutely reliable. It expands in communication, when information is added. It is negotiated with every new experience. To be in the process of communication means to be in the action of mapping—to be a map maker.

Andrea Blum is a professional map maker. Not by default, by being an artist—she's a map maker by inclination and choice. Her work maps out the private and the public, idiosyncrasies and pathologies, moods and memories. Being constructs in three dimensional space, her maps are immersive to an extent where they stop being maps, becoming environments and physical experiences, places for action.

#### the place

In Andrea Blum's work, arrangements and projects, the map and the territory sometimes overlap, sometimes frustrate, then again supplement each other. They are to be recognized, read and remembered. They sometimes disguise well. You happen into them. It's not like safely entering new ground after examining the orientation table first. Before you know it you find yourself sitting on it. The map and the territory concur in occupation, when the passer-by occurs. Their sensory quality is revealed in a strong appeal to our physical experience. To know how and where to be seated is relevant to them, to level your walk, to adjust your pace. With this work, only when you

very anti-monumental. In some ways they are tough and withholding in other ways they offer a generosity for other events to happen. The issue of scale in relation to voice has always been primary. How to work at a monumental scale without being dominant. My interest lies where the social, historical and psychological come together; what lies beneath the facade of generic, what dislocates site and content. Perhaps it is because of this that I am interested in how cities develop, how communities are formed and how sites are selected for art.

JK How do you yourself select a site for art? When the site is a given, how do you proceed to elect it for your piece or installation? Or do you claim it? Obviously you don't parachute the work. Which criteria interact with your selection, with the site that is selected: use, spatial qualities, architecture, light, traffic...?

AB Generally the sites are pre-selected. The 'program' of the work is the condition of the commissioner mixed with my own sensibility. Together a system is constructed which is enforced or denied depending on taste and context. That mix becomes 'selection/interpretation', which ultimately becomes 'strategy'.

< my personal interest lies where the social, historical and psychological come together

accept to be part of the map, to be included in the panorama that you perceive, can you expect to get significant information regarding your own presence and that of others. Whether on the scale of architecture or that of furniture, or even as a model, the work exists right on the edge of the private and the public. Upon the entry of its perceiver it is silently geared into motion. Its perspectives are opened to communication. Because it does not advertise as object, even less as *objet d'art*, it becomes a supportive environment to the play of orientation, on the promiscuous street ballet, the coded gallery show-down or elegant museum parade.

Andrea Blum's installations and projects are in more than one sense true 'civil works'. Both technically and culturally they engage in art and architecture as much as they do in street hassle, campus pamphletism, information nomadism or bourgeois decor. Her work amplifies the orientations of perception: map over matter being too ideological, matter over map proving too naive, nuances of map and matter meet in her spatial constructions. From a fascination with ritual exposure and interaction, with the mechanics and the psychologies of the 'peep hole', with framed, mapped perception, with exchanging information between cultures and idiosyncracies—all these articulated civil disturbances mark her interventions in the public and semi-public context.

Public presence has many different scales. We are tiny and anonymous when crossing a large, even empty, plaza but we can feel particularly uneasy in a crowded subway car. Agoraphobia and claustrophobia disable our presence. Social space is the reflex and construct that keeps us mobile. By 'educated guess' it measures the scale of particular public presence and guards the minimal proximity we allow others to come near. Its radius depends on the substantial context, on the spatial and material qualities of direct surroundings, on light conditions, on the feedback of information in reflections and shadows. But again social space is also informed by memory and media, by exemplary presence over time. Paranoia and other pathologies haunt all categories of presence and shred our maps to pieces.

Foremost the works of Andrea Blum celebrate the aesthetics of public performance in a full sense. Without being either nostalgic or cynical, they display pocket urban

I see myself as a respondent to clues which are already determined.
    When there is no particular site, I look for a site which can best catalyze the idea. In the project *Surveillance Station(s)*, in Den Haag, I selected the sites which marked the convergence of the city's histories in relation to its urban development. Each station, banquette, had a 180 degree panoramic mirror and map attached to a suspended structure. The mirror imaged the new city as the map charted the urban development of the city from 1370 to 1945. The viewer/public became witnesses to the past and future simultaneously. In contrast, the proposition for *Urban Loveseat* is designed for a generic bus stop or street seating. *Where* it is located is not as important as *how*. Working within a public context allows me to to consider more issues than concept and aesthetics. I am not interested in the notion of the masterpiece.
    Working with architecture allows me to establish a connection between life and art. I use a reductive architecture to be able to display the complex nuance of a situation. My work provides the conduit between what is seen and unseen.

1994, *Bunker*

Materials: Masonite, Plywood, Hardware
Dimensions: 185x215x125cm

Courtesy: Galerie des Archives, Paris

A love-seat is placed in an interior space. It is made of masonite, a material usually used for maquettes or prototypes. It is scaled to obscure the view of the companion except for the peep-hole which reveals the eyes of the other.

<the viewer/public became witnesses to the past and future simultaneously

landscapes with enough pressure points to alert a sensible user. Our public and private Janus faces are drawn to be invested into it. We are slowed down to focus on behavioural specificities. These places range in scale and reference from the architectural to the sculptural. Their affects range from the psychological to the political. They serve as a stage and as a passage. They fragment our glance to reassemble it under different angles. They awake the Passer-by to change his perception/action ratio, to perform the Voyeur, the Exhibitionist, the Loiterer, the Lurker, the Explorer; a Map Maker of sorts.

**information**

'The whole house with a roof, walls, windows and doors only lasts in fairy tales. Material and immaterial cables have penetrated it, have made Swiss cheese of it: antennae through the roof, telephone through the wall, television instead of windows and the car in a garage replacing the door.
    The whole house became a ruin, through which blow the blizzards of communication. (...) It calls for a new architecture, a new design.'

Vilém Flusser,
*Vom Stand der Dinge*

Myriad maps laying out one specific territory (even 'world')—that of mass media and specifically telecommunication—the past decennia have come to superimpose all other maps, to infect the intimacy of mind and body and curve our social space: its parameters 'puncturing holes in architecture'.

With the revolutionary technological acceleration of information media, all maps, all symbolic orders and reference systems will be impelled to update in Real Time. Presence and telepresence, representational simultaneity of different locations and the release of time zones into parallel time spans will challenge our maps to directly monitor the territories they claim to draw. Caught in informational drift we will spend at least as much but most likely more time on the map than in the turf. Information media becoming territories in their own right, hosting on-line communities and permitting the public exchange of every special interest imaginable, could drive the real world into museification, emptying it of its information, reconstructing it in computer networks, terminally tying us anonymously to its terminals.

Increasingly Andrea Blum's latter works, like *Surveillance Station(s)*, *Public Affairs* and *Information Plaza*, but already the never realized *Video Viewing Corridor* and *Newsstand* are designed to reconcile immediate experience and remote information, otherwise absent in time or space, now imported into the situation. Most recently *Information Plaza* (1996) on the campus of the Twente Technical University cautiously connects to the Internet and invites on-line interaction by electronic mail (lichtkrant@utwente.nl), its illuminated news trailers presenting local and global headlines 24 hours a day.

**JK** So the rules are provided by the context, by the user/viewer and by the work itself, however 'facilitary' it may be as a stage. It offers a limited amount of possibilities with which to interact. Each stage is different under different circumstances, people react differently in different sites. But there is a limit, a final rule, a line that is not crossed. Those are the rules of the street—anywhere except in the well-kept, well patrolled, well invested, well preserved areas.

**AB** My work has always incorporated the displacement of one set of information onto another whether it is a plaza, a garden or a piece of furniture. For example *Information Plaza*, at Twente University was a response to the university wanting a project which functioned as a meeting area and was environmentally considerate. It is a technical university with an international reputation for its research facilities. The university hosts many events and has visitors from all over the world. I used those specifics for the conceptual program of my project. Had it been a university which was more inwardly focused the art would have looked and functioned differently.
    It is interesting to think about the rules of the street versus the rules of art on the street. The street has so

1994, *Banquette*

Materials: Masonite, Plywood, Aluminum, Mirror, Hardware
Dimensions: 50x61x61cm each (edition of 10)

Courtesy: Galerie des Archives, Paris

Several chair modules are lined up in a row. They each have an aluminum framed vanity mirror attached to its structure.
As one sits in a chair, one's image is reflected in the mirror as well as the space around.

<my work has always incorporated the displacement of one set of information onto another

This particular piece both embodies a prominent site specificity—being a passage-cum-meeting point, having been built right on top of the University's major optical fiber and drainage pass—while displaying all the corporeal features of the civil work, including landscape elements, and is disconnected of its location through the visually dominating presence of immaterial information in bold green and red running LED displays. The culturally engineered qualities of some Dutch contemporary public art, as refereed by the Amsterdam based PBK Office for the Realisation of Public Projects of the Mondriaan Stichting (who also co-organized the *Plaza*), are challenged by Andrea Blum's investigations into the informationalization of the public sphere. An earlier (interior) installation in the Dutch context, *Public Affairs* (1995) for Stroom hcbk, crypto-domesticated the information of five years of public art commissioning by this institution. The exhibition design consisted of several pieces of linked or modular furniture-like objects/rooms, each conceived for a different representation of projects that themselves in many cases had been anti-monumental, temporary and ephemeral, now distributed in slides, sound, video, print, publications.

### home by conclusion

In Andrea Blum's installations one is not condoned to remain anonymous. One of their decisive qualities is to stage just these 'sets of practices' that, according to John Berger, can 'form one's home', enhance identity, give a name. The works afford interaction. They induce physical 'motor' memory, 'inscriptions' for our bodies which do not forget, and yet strongly advocate the forming of intelligent maps and communication systems that reveal the constructions of perception and the politics of presence.

While her public works of recent years more often than before connect to streams of information that span and neglect space and time, she also built *Domestic Arrangement* that focuses on intimacy, idiosyncrasy and privacy.

In her recent arrangements and projects the 'houses' of Berger, Bachelard and Flusser link to form places that map themselves and are truly democratic in the sense that they are anti-monumental, indeed like a home—a common place for exchange, in which information is vital and presence a predicament.

many levels of focus, from the most obvious to the virtually unnoticed. Choosing the method of interaction becomes a question of ego as much as a question of politics. It is true that in a well patrolled area work gains a type of protection, but often times, simultaneously, it loses its freedom to exist unselfconsciously. Since street life is impossible to control, the 'line that is not crossed' is impossible to designate. Because of this it is difficult to know the public, to know how public art functions. The puzzle is always unfinished and that is why it is interesting.

JK You allow the recipient of your work to 'happen into' it, but there are restrictions. What are they?

AB My work is direct. I employ a basic language in both the materials I use and the psychological/sociological conditions I impose. These conditions are not that extreme by nature. They become extreme when placed onto and into a different context. Sometimes the most interesting work is initially invisible. I like the surprise of being engaged in a project unknowingly. With my own work many people come and go without necessarily knowing that it is art. I renovated a pier in East Harlem, New York which, up until then, had been inaccessible for years.

1994, *Lure*

Materials: Masonite, Plywood,
Felt, Hardware
Dimensions: 137x245x125cm

A love seat is made of two
cubicles with a wall separating
each side.
The wall has an opening which
funtions as an arm rest for each
side scaled to expose only the
forearm of each occupant.
The entire interior space is lined
with grey fabric which cushions
the space and frames the
opening.

1994, Untitled (Neck)

Materials: Masonite, Plywood,
Felt, Hardware
Dimensions: 170x61x61cm

Courtesy: Galerie des Archives,
Paris

The back of the chair has a hole,
which allows for the view of the
back of the neck.
The hole is framed with an
industrial fabric which hangs
like a cape.

I'm sure 90% of the users had no idea that it was art but rather a place to hang out, an urban park. The important issue was that the city had invested in a poor neighbourhood giving the people a way to leave the city without leaving home. The fact that it was art had no meaning... the consequence of its public access did. Projects such as these play an interesting game with one's own ego. The restrictions are those that you impose on yourself... what you are willing to do in a public situation... what is too embarrassing, too exposing, too compromising.

A woman on the street navigates differently from a man. Looking in the shop window at your reflection is not just vanity, but a check on personal security as well. The street pieces (public pieces) refer to situations that are always in flux... access, navigation, watching, passing through... I work with the transition/transportation through this space. I layer the private space onto the public space of access. I present an incident or locate a pressure point . The complete dynamic is idiosyncratic and immaterial. I try not to compete with the urban complexity but rather I attempt to use the work to footnote the subliminal voice.

JK When one stops in this flux one becomes vulnerable, to ones own perception and/or to influences from out-

1994, *Body Image*

Materials: Masonite, Plywood,
Mirrored Stainless Steel,
Hardware
Dimensions: 107x107x61cm

Courtesy: Galerie des Archives,
Paris

The interior of the chair is lined
with mirrored stainless steel
reflecting the image of the body,
and the surrounding room, within
its structure.

<a woman on the street navigates differently from a man

**18**

1996, *La Chambre de Christophe Durand-Ruel* Rue Bonaparte, Paris

Materials: Plywood, 20mm Plexiglas, Aluminum, Fluorescent Lights (8) Room size 275x450x250cm

Courtesy: Galerie des Archives, Paris

A small bedroom is in the apartment of a collector/gallerist in Paris. The 'art' is the room itself, designed for the special needs of the occupant. The room is covered in a shell of wood converting it into a type of box in which a built-in bed and two night tables are installed. A clear plexiglas bureau is built wall-to-wall and is illuminated with flourescent lights, exposing the personal affairs of the collector. Attached to the walls are shelves which flip up or down depending on the amount of items he wishes to display.

side, to another person's objectifying gaze. Isn't the street a hostile place for the art and its viewer?

**AB** The street is simultaneously hostile and protective. Anonymity can be a protective blanket which again questions the decision of making a monument or inscribing a notation. I am interested in art that could survive the museum or the mall. One arena is not better than the other, but each demands a different approach. What that approach is, and how it differs from one context to another is how the program is tested.

*Public Affairs* was an exhibition commissioned by Stroom hcbk to present projects of other artists which had been commissioned by Stroom during the last five years. The installation design was staged to place the viewer/public in a situation which combined the program of the institution with my own needs as an artist. The public was placed in various intimate situations in the public space of the exhibition hall.

**JK** So when the art 'creeps around' the public, what happens if one becomes aware? *Public Affairs* showed a delicate balance between the documentation, its presentation and your installation. One could focus in and out of

< anonymity can be a protective blanket

1996, *La Chambre de Christophe Durand-Ruel* Rue Bonaparte, Paris

these qualities, shift attention. The furniture-like pieces literally fold around you, offer a refuge—until you discover that part of you is exposed to another person's gaze.

**AB** They are scaled to be a cross between a large chair and a small room as they address the mystery of attraction. Two people sit side by side in a felt-padded booth, the forearm of each occupant is in view, while the person's identity remains anonymous. Whether the pieces 'view' the back of the neck, the upper leg, the eyes, or the side of the head they allow me to use architecture in a narrative way.

The context for these projects vary. *Domestic Arrangement* was a series of exhibitions in Paris, Amsterdam and New York which attempted to convert the gallery into a furniture showroom made up of pieces which functioned as furniture. Some are designed for the home, others are made for the semi-public space of the bank, the waiting room, the lobby. Ideally, if one were in a museum they could be used to relax in and look at other art. One could be in one piece of art looking at another piece of art. I would love the museum to become more accessible and interactive with its public, for the museum to be a kind of home away from home, a refuge, a place of

<two people sit side by side in a felt-padded booth, the forearm of each occupant is in view

1996, *Mobile Home*

Material: MDF

Courtesy: Galerie des Archives,
Paris

*Mobile Home* is made up of a
collection of modular structures
that assemble and re-assemble,
like a massive 'tinkertoy'.
Its parts locate the private and
social spaces of the home using a
formally spare, yet
psychologically complex method
of arrangement.
It comes apart, is compact,
transportable, cheap to construct,
and can change configuration to
accommodate business and
domestic needs.

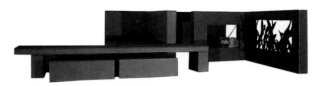

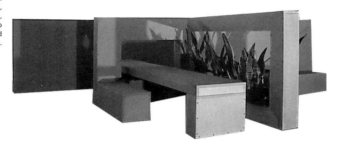

comfort. I would like my work to function as an agent to position and de-position, from one context to another.

**JK** Why does it need reductiveness of architectural form to identify a subtext? You don't want the architectural qualities of your work to enhance the promiscuity of interaction?

**AB** The reductiveness of the form allows for the complexity of the 'peep hole'.

**JK** Today the social is displaced between the private and the public. Constantly we see the function of space and of the institutions that are housed in architectural space shift. Will we one day have to leave home, in order to be private, when our places are so invaded by media and information that we can no longer live in them? Is privacy only guaranteed in anonymity—being private equaling being unknown, without a name? Do we leave a trace when we cruise the street, in avoidance of our houses that are invaded with ghostly media imagery?

1996, *Mobile Home*

'We live in a mobile time as we move out of one life into another. Our sense of how to live is now dominated by the economy of possessions in relation to the economy of space.
We are urban nomads, constantly on the move because of escalating real estate prices or change of work. Economics coupled with urban development have reduced our needs as it squeezes us into domestic spaces half the size of what we are used to, out of the neighborhoods we grew up in'

< I would like my work to function as an agent to position and de-position

1996, *Mobile Home*

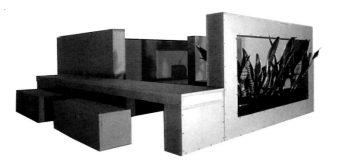

**AB** Fifteen years ago the street had a different function. It was an arena for walking, lingering, sexual pick-ups, amusement. Now there is no time to linger, AIDS.has made the sexual street ballet obsolete, homelessness has claimed the sites of amusement. Street life has become neutered. People on the street are afraid. They are afraid for their safety, afraid of being late, afraid of witnessing an event which confronts their own conscience.

**JK** So the public pieces slow down the public pace to freeze frame speed... slow us down until we sit down, puzzled, to investigate...

**AB** I think of the work as functioning as a slowed down cinema strip where all the details become the text/narrative—how rules are made and broken, and how rhythms get started and shifted.

**JK** A space or stage or installation that is not advertising itself as art will still represent a difference, something other than facility, other than street furniture. This alerts the viewer, opens some of them to experience. This is

< fifteen years ago the street had a different function

1995, *Public Affairs*

Stroom hcbk
Den Haag, the Netherlands

Courtesy: Lumen Travo,
Amsterdam

1995, *Image Bench*

Materials: MDF, Plexiglas.
Fluorescent Lights, Duratrans
Dimensions: 150x125x125cm

*Public Affairs* is an exhibition design conceived as a conduit between the domestic and the public.
Working from and into the architectural axis's of the room seven 'furniture' units were designed to convert the exhibition space into a display for Stroom's history as well as for viewer/public behavior. The 'art' becomes the body for existing information of other commissioned works as it addresses ideas about leisure, intimacy, and voyeurism in a public space exposed to public view.

what 'art' does. Your work is quite easily perceived as 'different' even without necessarily being advertised as 'art'. All that is this kind of different asks for our attention. That seems to be too noncommittal—but there are 'rules' at work that do in a sense (quietly) dominate the situations in which your works emerge. Pressure points force the recipients gaze in a specific direction and give it a quality.

**AB** Every situation has its own set of rules. The *Sunken Network System* in San Francisco had three navigation systems which were designed to reconnect the site to the surrounding community. *Benches & Walkways* charted and replaced the University navigation system with that of the students, offering the possibility of the continuous redesign of the campus in relation to student needs.

In the large scale public pieces there are network systems and passages with architectural pressure points. In the furniture pieces the parts of the body are the pressure points.

**JK** The idea of slowing down, in order to allow the reversal of the text and the subtext is a powerful mechanism

Material: MDF
Dimensions: 150x125x125cm

< in the furniture pieces the parts of the body are the pressure points

1995, *Desk*

Materials: MDF,
Fluorescent Lights
Dimensions: 150x85x125cm

1995, *Park Bench*

Material: MDF
Dimensions: 125x75x400cm

to enhance. The scale of the interface changes with the spatial and psychological environment, context, even mood... also the spatial mood—the mood of material, texture, light, volume and distance. Space could collapse, like in step motion cinematography, or freeze frame.

**AB** There is a film by Kurasawa done, in 1970, called 'DoDesKaDen'. In one section two drunk men, living in the slum area of Tokyo, try to find their way home. The shanties all look alike except for some distinct coloration. Each man tries to find his way home by color matching his head-band to a shanty until he finds one that matches. Urban spaces are designed without distinction. Housing complexes have replaced neighborhoods, airports have been converted into shopping malls. As with the film, we search for clues to find our way home.

**JK** To find our way home means to venture outside of it—to 'match our headbands' in the wild and implement changing sets of practices. This reminds me of a text by John Berger who says that home is represented by a set of practices rather than a house. These practices, he says, are chosen and not imposed, that, home is no longer

Materials: MDF, Plexiglas,
Fluorescent Lights, (Sound)
Dimensions: 125x475x70cm

< we search for clues to find our way home

1995, *Video Viewing Station*

Material: MDF
Dimensions: 175x675x225cm

a dwelling but the untold story of a life being lived.

**AB** The habits of domestic life are transposed onto the street. How we walk, talk, eat, relax is negotiated onto the scale of the public site. We leave our home and carry it like a backpack throughout the day. We take it with us out to the street, the theatre, the subway, the mall. We take our walls, chairs, libraries and vanities with us. We put on a coat and think of it as a warm bath. We buy a newspaper to fit around us like a mobile home. We sit in the park and find the same seat as yesterday. We drink a coffee to make the public space our living room. We take a train and get under the covers of the book. We wear sunglasses to separate our room from another. We look in car windows to try to locate our reflection in a context. We cross the street and try to remember why we left home.

New York 12-13 October 1995

1995, *Video Viewing Station*

< we drink a coffee to make the public space our living room

1996, *Information Plaza*

Site: Twente University,
Enschede, the Netherlands
Materials: Cast Concrete, Water,
Fluorescent Lights, Boulders,
LED Headline System
(via the Internet)
Dimensions structure:
2,5x24x22m;
with paths: 2,5x9x51m

Sponsor: Twente University;
Mondriaan Stichting,
Amsterdam, the Netherlands

Courtesy: Lumen Travo,
Amsterdam

Two squares overlap in the middle of the campus of a technical university in eastern Holland. The resulting structure mirrors the adjacent architecture in position and attributes. A multi-level public space is created for the display of news which is accessed to the Internet and which runs continuously.

The interior walls of the upper level of this structure are encircled by a fragmented flow of green LED that display regional and university news in Dutch. This display is accompanied by built-in bench structures that position the viewer/public in an intimate relationship to each other and to the news itself.

The exterior walls of the lower level, display national and international news, in all languages, in red LED. These walls contain rock and water that connect to the water system of the campus as a whole

The pavilion/plaza structure is penetrated by a bicycle path that connects to the existing path common to the university, establishing a central space for the university accessible from all directions.

**38**

1995, *Camouflage*

Site: Metrobus Petit Quevilly,
SIVOM de l'agglomeration
Rouenaise, Rouen, France
Material: Perforated Steel
Dimensions: 4,0 x1,3x1,3m

Sponsor: Direction Régionale
des Affaires Culturelles
de Haute-Normandie
Courtesy: Galerie des Archives,
Paris

A pole forms the conceptual
linkage of a multiple of stations
of a new Metrobus system in
Rouen.This pole functions as the
central spine of a 4-way seating
structure made of perforated
steel. The holes create a
'camouflage' which
simultaneously hides and
exposes one traveler
from another.
The intimacy of this social space
is enhanced by the 'peep holes'
which both clarifies the view and
enforces the barrier.

**40**

1992, *Surveillance Station(s)*

Site: Den Haag, the Netherlands
(temporary installation)
Materials: Cast Concrete, Steel,
Aluminum, Plexiglas,
Fluorescent Lights,
Convex Mirror, Silkscreen
Dimensions: each 2,7x1,5x0,9m
Sponsor: Stroom hcbk,
Den Haag, the Netherlands

Courtesy: Lumen Travo,
Amsterdam

The siting of five *Surveillance
Stations* mark the juncture of the
historical layers of urban
development while attempting to
address the city as a city in the
process of change.
The public is placed as
watchdogs to that change. It is
seated facing the old city, while
the new city is viewed in 180
degree panoramic distortion from
behind, placed overhead, framing
the view in front.
A graphic image of the changing
development of the city from the
14th to the mid twentieth century
is mapped onto the back side of
the suspended light box locating
and illuminating the
viewer/station.

## Gesprek tussen Andrea Blum en Jouke Kleerebezem

**JK** Veel hedendaagse kunst in de openbare ruimte lijkt het monumentale te hebben verruild voor investeringen in een mense-lijke schaal en in menselijk handelen. Een monument dwingt aandacht af, gebiedt nederigheid, niet direkt betrokkenheid. Monumenten ondersteunen meestal de dominante ideologie. Ze leggen beslag op openbare ruimte, en bieden daarbij geen 'podium' voor onderhandeling en uitwisseling van informatie, voor het individuele geheugen, voor sociaal-culturele interactie, of sexualiteit. In jouw werk blijft een monumentale, architecturale schaal behouden zonder dat het ons onderdrukt.

**AB** Mij interesseren eerder de 'tussenruimten' dan de monumenten, ruimte die ontworpen werd voor aankomst en vertrek, ont-snapping en beschutting. Het trottoir, een doorgang, een wachtruimte zijn zulke onderdelen van een architectuur, die haar ondersteunen maar binnen haar hiërarchie onzichtbaar blijven. Ik presenteer mijn werken nooit als monumenten, ze zijn juist anti-monumentaal. Enerzijds zijn ze hard en ontoegankelijk, anderzijds ook genereus en gastvrij voor een mogelijk gebruik. De

< mij interesseren de 'tussenruimten' in de monumenten

1992, *Surveillance Station(s)*

verhouding tussen de schaal en de uitdrukkingskracht van het werk is altijd zeer belangrijk geweest: hoe hanteer je, op elk niveau in het werk een monumentale maat zonder te domineren? Mij fascineert het als sociale, historische en psychologische effecten elkaar ontmoeten: wat verschuilt zich achter de façade van de algemeenheid, hoe raken plekken en hun inhoud ontregeld? Daarom interesseert het me waarschijnlijk ook hoe stedelijke ruimte zich ontwikkelt, hoe deze groeit, hoe zich gemeenschappen vormen en op basis waarvan we dan plekken voor de kunst selecteren.

**JK** Hoe kies je zelf een plek voor je werk? Als hij gegeven is zul je hem voor je werk of installatie moeten verbijzonderen—of neem je een plek volledig in bezit? Het is duidelijk dat je je werk niet domweg 'parachuteert'. Wat speelt er mee in het verbijzonderen van een gegeven plek tot dé plek voor je werk: het gebruik, de architectuur, ruimtelijke, landschappelijke kwaliteiten, licht, verkeer...?

**AB** Over het algemeen is de plek gegeven. Mijn 'programma' bestaat hierin dat ik de randvoorwaarden onder invloed van mijn ervaring en interesse interpreteer. Dan ontstaat een nieuw systeem van voorwaarden, dat vervolgens in het werk wordt versterkt, of ontkend, al naar gelang de specifieke lokatie naar mijn idee nodig heeft. Uit de vermenging van 'selektie/interpretatie'

< mij fascineert het als sociale, historische en psychologische effecten elkaar ontmoeten

**44**

1992, *Corporate Displacement*

Site: General Mills Corporate
Headquarters, Minneapolis MN
Materials: Terrazzo, Glass, Mirror,
Aluminum, Fluorescent Lights,
Golden Flame Spirea
(Landscape Material)
Dimensions: South Courtyard
(Pavilions) 3x24x18m
North Courtyard (Boardroom)
1.7x9x18m

Sponsor: General Mills
Corporation, Inc.

Two modernist buildings are
intercepted by a third forming an
'H' configuration.
Each subsequent courtyard is
equal in placement and visual
access to the landscaped ground
of the corporate headquarters.
The two sides share material and
form, and address the concept of
'corporate displacement'.

The South Courtyard, the larger
of the two, displaces the 'module'
of the building, or interior office
space, to the exterior, becoming
two garden pavilions. The walls
are the same black glass as the
building skin though are louvered
to distort and break up the image
of the sanctuary and those within
it. These pavilions are placed at
the end of a narrow walkway
which projects out from the
upper level and connects to the
building corridor. The elevated
open space becomes a type of
'back porch' with banquettes
placed upon it.

The North Courtyard takes the
idea of the 'corporate boardroom'
and places it outside to become a
public meeting space. The scale
of the long table and eight chairs
implies a perverse architecture
which is heightened by the
interior mirrors of the chairs
reflecting the occupant(s) in
mutiple images.

van de plek ontstaat een strategie. Bestaande voorwaarden bieden aanwijzingen van waaruit zich het werk ontwikkelt.

Zijn er geen duidelijke richtlijnen, dan zoek ik zelf plekken die mijn ideeën het beste op gang brengen. In *Surveillance Station(s)*, het projekt dat ik in Den Haag uitvoerde, koos ik voor die plekken waar de geschiedenis van de stad op stedelijke vernieuwing botste. Elk 'station', elk bankje, dat zicht op een historische plek bood, droeg een panoramaspiegel waarin je recente stadsonwikkelingsprojekten weerspiegeld zag, met daar achterop een plattegrond van de stedebouwkundige ontwikkelingen in de periode 1370 tot 1945. Het publiek, de gebruiker, ervoer letterlijk in een oogopslag een historische en de eigentijdse stad.
    In tegenstelling tot dit werk is *Urban Loveseat* (dat nooit uitgevoerd werd) ontworpen als een doodgewoon bushalte-bankje. Waar het staat is minder belangrijk dan hoe het geconstrueerd is. Het werk in de openbare ruimte laat naast conceptuele en esthetische overwegingen ook andere toe. Passanten worden in de *Urban Loveseat* in een ongebruikelijke verhouding tot elkaar geplaatst. Het toepassen van architektonische elementen maakt het mogelijk verbindingen tussen het dagelijks leven en de kunst te leggen, waarbij mijn werk tussen de zichtbare en onzichtbare regels van de openbaarheid bemiddelt. Mijn teruggehouden vormentaal is dienstbaar aan de genuanceerde complexiteit van de openbaarheid.

< het toepassen van architektonische elementen maakt het mogelijk verbindingen tussen het dagelijks leven en de kunst te leggen

# Gemeengoed, plaats, informatie

'...home is represented, not by a house, but by a practice, or by a set of practices. Everyone has his own. These practices, chosen and not imposed, offer in their repetition, transient as they may be in themselves, more permanence, more shelter than any lodging. Home is no longer a dwelling but the untold story of a life being lived. At its most brutal, home is no more than one's name...'

John Berger
*And our faces, my heart, brief as photos*

## gemeengoed

Kennis verschilt van plaats tot plaats, zij straalt in lokale kleuren. Onze directe ervaring is net zo plaatsgebonden. Op basis van de omgang met karakteristieke plekken stelt onze geest een veelheid aan kaarten en plattegronden samen. Deze is even veelzijdig als de keur aan topografische, economische, ecologische, demografische, bodemkundige en andere kaarten, die van willekeurig welk gebied is op te maken. Onze kaarten volgen over het algemeen de geldende regels en sturen onze intuïtie aan de hand van suggestieve symbolen en afbeeldingen. De kaart interpreteert en kleurt het gebied. Conventionele informatiebemiddeling, zoals die van de massamedia, onderdrukt de eigengereide mogelijkheden van de gewone kaartenmaker, van 'Jan met de Kaart'. Maar ook gemedialiseerde informatie wordt door ons ingebed en begrepen vanuit de dagelijkse omgeving waarvan we ons de plattegrond eigen maakten. Vreemde kaarten tasten volgens sommigen de intimiteit van deze omgeving aan, door onze ervaring in een roes te brengen, maar reflexen beheersen nog steeds onze gewoontepraktijken, de 'sets of practices, zoals John Berger ze noemt.

We leren onze eigen kaarten—die nooit met het terrein samenvallen, maar dit dankzij hun beeldende kracht wel in belangrijke mate vormen—te accepteren als blauwdrukken voor onze waarneming en daarmee voor onze motoriek. Kaarten schotelen ons patronen voor en geven soms gedetailleerde informatie over de omstandigheden waarin we ons bevinden. Zo maken ze onze mobiliteit afhankelijk. Blind volgt deze de sporen van de kaartenmaker en ontzegt zich daarmee de verovering van de werkelijkheid op de kaart. Verborgen legenden en wèl in het oog springende indrukken spelen een luchtig spel met ons motorieke systeem, dat de ene voet voor de andere plaatst, een lach op ons gezicht trekt, kippevel zaait, of onze hand op de tast leidt om de huid en de weerstand te ervaren van de materiële werkelijkheid waaruit onze omgeving is samengesteld.

Navigeren leren we door ervaring, toetsing, in kaart brengen. We informeren onze kaarten door voortdurend 'sets of practices', gewoontepraktijken, in te voeren. Zulke aanpassingen aan de hand van onze levensloop slaan we

**JK** De context stelt dus regels, zowel ingegeven door bevooroordeeldheid, bij de gebruiker, als doordat het werk de context vergroot. Hoe facilitair en dienstbaar het er in eerste instantie als 'podium' ook uitziet, het biedt slechts een beperkt aantal mogelijkheden. De podia verschillen per plek en veranderen in hun gebruik, op die specifieke lokatie, maar er is altijd een grens aan de mogelijkheden: die wordt gevormd door de 'regels van de straat', die overal gelden (behalve misschien in goed onderhouden en gesurveilleerde, goed gefinancierde geprivilegieerde wijken).

**AB** In mijn werk heb ik altijd verschillende soorten informatie met elkaar vergeleken, of het nu in een plein, een tuin of een stuk meubilair gestalte kreeg. *Information Plaza* bijvoorbeeld, op de campus van de TU Twente, beantwoordt aan de vraag van de opdrachtgever om een ontmoetingsplek, om een werk ook dat 'milieu bewust' was. De onderzoeksfaciliteitenze van deze technische universiteit genieten een internationale reputatie. Er worden veel activiteiten ontplooid die gasten van over de hele wereld trekken. Die gegevens werden door mij in het concept verwerkt. Als het een universiteit was geweest met een veel beslotener programma dan had de kunst er anders uitgezien en gefunctioneerd.

Wat de straat betreft: het is interessant hoe de regels van de straat zich verhouden tot de regels van kunst op straat. Het straat-

1992, *Split Pavilion*

Site: Ocean Boulevard,
Carlsbad CA
Materials: Cast Concrete,
Galvanized Steel Railing, Water,
Light, Landscape Material
Dimensions: 3m high, 930sqm

Sponsor: City of Carlsbad
Department of Cultural Arts

A wedge shape space becomes
an overlook to the Pacific Ocean.
The street side runs adjacent to
a highway along the coastline.
Responding to the moving
vehicular traffic, forming a
cinematic-scrim, is a high steel
rail structure establishing a
partition from the street.
This structure opens at the
center of the wedge to project
towards the ocean forming a
trellis for what ultimately
becomes a split pavilion.

The pavilion is cut in two by a
water trough which runs
perpendicular to the ocean,
culminating in a central pool.
Illusionistically the water 'lifts'
the ocean to its own level
forming the conceptual fulcrum
of the overall project. From this
central point the other elements
emanate; the landscape is
raised, the walkways sink; the
structure breaks down onto an
area of access. The lighting is
built into the water
redistributing the gravitational
'weight' of the project from
day to night.

< in mijn werk heb ik altijd verschillende soorten informatie met elkaar vergeleken

zorgvuldig op om als referentie te dienen voor blinde vlekken op de kaart, voor nieuwe plaatsen en andere openbaarheden. De informatie die we aanspreken om de straat over te steken—als we om het even welke langgerekte ruimte tussen twee rijen huizen overbruggen, of het nu een modderig pad of vier banen asfalt is—deze navigatie informatie onttrekken we aan een eindeloos bestand overtochten: die van onszelf, van onze familie, van buren en vrienden en de vele die door de media op de kaart werden gezet. Elke nieuwe oversteek verrijkt dit bestand.

'...the house we were born in has engraved within us the hierarchy of the various functions of inhabiting. We are the diagram of the functions of inhabiting that particular house, and all the other houses are but variations on a fundamental theme. The word habit is too worn a word to express this passionate liaison of our bodies, which do not forget, with an unforgettable house.'

Gaston Bachelard
*The Poetics of Space*

Voorbij het opnamevermogen van ons geheugen worden, volgens Gaston Bachelard, ruimtes 'fysiek in ons gegrift', als 'groepen organische gewoontes'. Hij beschrijft de herinnering aan het huis uit onze kindertijd als een onvergetelijke lichamelijke, letterlijk vormende ervaring. Zonder dergelijke indrukken ontbreekt het ons aan informatie en vallen we terug op gemeenplaatsen. De gemeenplaats is een verstek laten gaan. Hij weerspiegelt de aanvaarding van een status quo waarin geen informatie wordt toegevoegd. Hij leidt tot stilstand of hooguit plichtmatige beweging. De gemeenplaats vernietigt de verbeelding en maakt iedere kaart overbodig. De kwaliteiten die Bachelard aan het 'particular house of childhood' toekent kennen we ook van andere plekken die een onuitwisbare indruk achterlieten. Plekken die geen gemeenplaatsen waren griften bewegingen in onze mobiliteit, waarmee de kennis van onze omgeving werd gevoed.

De uitgekiende kaart heeft verbeeldingskracht, is intelligent en gevoelig, zowel tastbaar als grafisch, zodat we hem, als we ons onder nieuwe omstandigheden bevinden, voor de geest kunnen halen. Het in kaart gebrachte geheugen is echter als een bibliotheek zonder al te deugdelijk register, een complex systeem van referenties, dat we evenwel absoluut betrouwbaar achten. Het breidt zich onder invloed van informatietoevoer uit. Het wordt bij elke nieuwe ervaring geraadpleegd: communiceren betekent in kaart brengen, kaartenmaker zijn.

Andrea Blum is een professionele kaartenmaker. Niet zonder meer omdat ze kunstenaar is, maar van nature en uit eigen keuze. Haar werken brengen privéomgevingen en openbare ruimtes in kaart, overgevoeligheden en ziektebeelden, stemmingen en herinneringen. Omdat het driedimensionale konstrukties zijn nemen haar kaarten

---

leven heeft vele niveaus waarop je je kunt concentreren. Je keuze voor een vorm van interactie of interventie baseer je op zelfstandige en politieke overwegingen. Ongetwijfeld geniet het kunstwerk in goed gesurveilleerde wijken een zekere bescherming, die echter ten koste van zijn vanzelfsprekendheid gaat. Omdat het straatleven zich niet laat controleren zijn de grenzen die het aan het kunstwerk stelt absoluut niet aan te geven. Om die reden is het moeilijk om je publiek te kennen en blijft ook het functioneren van kunst in de openbare ruimte moeilijk te analyseren. Het is een onopgelost vraagstuk en dat maakt het voor mij nu juist zo interessant.

JK Tot op zekere hoogte laat je de passant terloops in het werk opgenomen worden, maar je stelt ook beperkingen. Welke?

AB Mijn werk is direct. Ik hanteer zowel in het materiaalgebruik als in de sociaal-psychologische voorwaarden die het werk stelt een eenvoudige grammatika. Het werk biedt geen extreme mogelijkheden, die ontstaan vanzelf in de wisselwerking met de context. Het interessantste werk is soms in eerste instantie onvindbaar... Ik houd wel van de verrassing die je ervaart als je ineens in een werk blijkt te zijn beland! Mensen komen en gaan in mijn eigen werk, ze zijn zich niet noodzakelijkerwijs bewust dat het kunst is. De pier die ik in East Harlem renoveerde was een aantal jaren ontoegankelijk geweest. Negentig procent van de gebrui-

1991, *107th St Pier*
In cooperation with architects
Giorgio Cavaglieri & Joseph Sultan

Site: East River, New York City
Materials: Concrete, Terrazzo,
Steel, Lights
Dimensions: 4,26x75x18,28m

Sponsor: New York City
Percent for Art Program &
Public Development Corporation

A pier is sited in the East River of New York City. It was built in 1939 to accomodate the practical needs of the then active river industry. Abandoned with the advent of the East River Drive it fell into disrepair until the City saw it as an opportunity to restore it for recreational use as an urban park.

The project is an attempt to reengage the site with the East Harlem Community as well as the larger layout of the City.
A series of framing devices are built into the project in both structure as well as flat surfaces.

<je keuze voor een vorm van interactie of interventie basseer je op zelfstandige en politieke overwegingen

**58**

ons op, zodat we ze op een gegeven moment niet meer als plattegrond ervaren maar als omgeving, als plaats van handeling.

### plaats

In het werk van Andrea Blum komt het voor dat de kaart en het gebied elkaar overlappen, dat ze elkaar aanvullen, maar ook dat ze elkaar in de weg zitten. Het werk moet herkend, gelezen en herinnerd worden. Soms ligt het goed verscholen en overvalt het je. Het is meestal niet zo geconstrueerd dat je je er rustig op kunt oriënteren voordat je je erin begeeft. Kaart en gebied raken verbonden zodra er zich een voorbijganger aandient die de omgeving in bezit probeert te nemen. De zintuigelijke kwaliteiten van het werk ervaar je aan de fysieke voorwaarden die het stelt. Hoe en waar te zitten is van belang, net als je loop aanpassen, en je tempo. Alleen als je accepteert dat je in dit werk een onderdeel van de kaart bent, opgenomen in het panorama dat je waarneemt, kun je betekenisvolle informatie verwachten over je eigen aanwezigheid en die van anderen. Zowel in een architektonische maatvoering, als in die van het meubilair—zelfs in de modellen—functioneert het werk precies op de scheiding van de privéomgeving en de openbaarheid. Zodra de gebruiker zich aandient komt het werk als het ware in beweging en opent het een perspektief op communicatie. Omdat het werk zichzelf niet als objekt presenteert, en nog minder als kunstobjekt, wordt het de geëigende omgeving voor het spel van de oriëntatie, op de promiscuïteit van het straatleven, de geserreerde krachtmetingen in de galerie of de elegante museale parade.

Andrea Blum's installaties en werken in de openbare ruimte zijn in meer dan één betekenis 'civiele werken'. Ze hebben evenzeer betrekking op kunst en architektuur als op het straatleven, het pamflettisme van de campus, ons informatienomadisme of de burgerlijke interieurkunst. Het werk versterkt ons oriëntatievermogen. De kaart wordt niet als belangrijker dan het terrein gepresenteerd (dat zou te ideologisch zijn), het terrein ook niet boven de kaart verheven (wat te naïef zou zijn). In genuanceerde gebaren verzoent het werk—al is het maar tijdelijk— kaart en terrein. Andrea Blum's interventies in de (semi-) openbaarheid worden gekarakteriseerd door haar fascinatie met rituele onthulling en interactie, met de mechanismen en psychologieën van de 'peephole', met een ingekaderde, in kaart gebrachte waarneming, met de

---

kers had er geen notie van dat het een kunstwerk was. Het werd weer een plek om rond te hangen, een soort klein stedelijk park. Het belangrijkste was nog wel dat de stad weer eens in een arme buurt had geïnvesteerd en mensen de gelegenheid gaf 'de stad uit te gaan zonder hun huis te verlaten'... Het feit dat het een kunstwerk was had geen betekenis... dat de pier weer toegankelijk was des te meer.

Je ego wordt in zulke projekten aardig op de proef gesteld. De meeste beperkingen leg je jezelf op... waartoe ben je in het openbaar bereid... wat ervaar je als genant, te exhibitionistisch, compromitterend? Dergelijke beperkingen komen uit de eigen neurosen voort. Een vrouw beweegt zich anders over straat dan een man. Een blik in de winkelruit wordt niet ingegeven door ijdelheid: je controleert je omgeving... Mijn werken op straat verwijzen altijd naar die staat van voortdurende verandering: je verschaft je toegang, oriënteert je, kijkt, bent onherroepelijk een passant... Ik stapel de individuele sociale ruimte van mensen bovenop de openbare ruimte die ze betreden. Ik breng ergens een nieuw detail aan of construeer een knelpunt. De dynamiek blijft eigengereid en is immaterieel. Ik concurreer niet met de de stedelijke complexiteit, het werk is een voetnoot, met een subtiele uitdrukkingskracht en effect.

1992, *Surveillance Marquee*

Site: Rue des Archives, Paris
Materials: Stainless Steel,
Convex Plexiglas Mirror
Dimensions: each 36x47x18cm

Courtesy: Galerie des Archives,
Paris

Seven units are placed around
the exterior of a gallery space in
Paris. Their placement is in relation to the architectural columns
of the building itself, as it occupies
the intersection of two streets.
The units are stainless steel box-
like shapes with convex mirrors
inset on each side, giving them a
double-curved profile; a cross
between the classical street lamp
and contemporary television
monitor. Each unit projects
outward from the side of the
building at progressive intervals.
The viewer/passerby is reflected
coming and going in two
directions simultaneously.
The reflections of street life and
gallery life become interwoven.

<een vrouw beweegt zich anders over straat dan een man

**60**

informatieuitwisseling tussen culturele en individuele overgevoeligheden; met andere woorden, door de articulatie van civiele ongemakken.

Onze aanwezigheid in het openbaar kent verschillende schaalverhoudingen. We zijn klein en anoniem als we een groot plein oversteken, vooral als het leeg is, maar we kunnen ons enorm (en) ongemakkelijk voelen in een overvolle tram. Plein- en engtevrees hinderen onze tegenwoordigheid. Het instandhouden van een zogenaamde 'sociale ruimte' houdt ons in veel gevallen op de been. Het bepaalt de minimale afstand waarop we anderen in onze nabijheid dulden. De straal van de sociale ruimte is echter niet alleen afhankelijk van psychologische en sociale factoren, maar ook van de ruimtelijke en materiële kwaliteit van de omgeving, van lichtomstandigheden, van het informatiegehalte van spiegelbeelden en schaduwen. Weer spelen de herinnering en de media een rol. Zij leveren voorbeelden van presentie. Maar daarnaast belagen achtervolgingswaanzin en andere angsten ons zelfbeeld en scheuren ze onze plattegronden aan stukken.

Het werk van Andrea Blum heeft nog een belangrijke kwaliteit. Het viert ten volle de esthetiek van ons openbare functioneren. Zonder in nostalgie of cynisme te vervallen biedt het ons kleine stedelijke landschappen waarin zich voldoende knelpunten bevinden om de wakkere passant te alarmeren. Het betrekt onze privaat/ openbare Januskop in het verhaal. Het vertraagt onze gang opdat we ons in gedragskundige details kunnen verdiepen. De projekten variëren in schaal, van architecturaal tot sculpturaal. Hun toegenegenheid is zowel psychologisch als politiek. Ze dienen tot podium en doorgang. Ze breken onze blik in stukken om hem onder een andere hoek weer in elkaar te zetten. Ze roepen de passant op om de verhouding waarneming/handeling te veranderen: een Voyeur te worden, een Exhibitionist, een Lummelaar, of Verkenner, en zeker: een Kaartenmaker.

informatie

Een explosieve hoeveelheid kaarten verleent de laatste decennia een geheel nieuw gebied betekenis: de wereld van de massamedia en meer in het bijzonder van de telecommunicatie. Haar plattegronden bedekken alle andere. Ze overdonderen de intimiteit van onze dagelijkse omgevingen en buigen de curven van onze sociale ruimten af.

JK Als je halt houdt wordt je kwetsbaar, je wordt je je rol als waarnemer bewust en je ervaart invloeden van buitenaf, voor de objectiverende blik van de ander. Is de straat geen vijandige plek voor de kunst en zijn liefhebbers?

AB De straat is vijandig èn biedt bescherming. Anonimiteit kan bescherming bieden. Dit stelt ook de vraag aan de orde of je een monument op moet richten of een soort inscriptie achterlaten. Mij interesseert juist de kunst die zowel het museum als het winkelcentrum overleeft. De ene context is niet superieur aan de andere, elk vraagt om een andere aanpak. Welke die is, en waarin de contexten precies verschillen: daaraan toets je je programma.

*Public Affairs* was bijvoorbeeld een tentoonstelling waartoe Stroom hcbk opdracht gaf. De opdracht luidde om hun activiteiten op het gebied van kunst in de openbare ruimte van de jaren 1991-1995 in de eigen tentoonstellingsruimte te presenteren. Ik ontwierp een installatie die het programma van het instituut toetste aan mijn eigen ideeën en verlangens: in de openbaarheid van de tentoonstellingsruimte werd het publiek op verschillende manieren in intieme situaties geplaatst.

JK Wat gebeurt er wanneer een publiek zich bewust wordt dat het zich door het werk laat 'inpakken'? *Public Affairs* bood nog

1993 , *Video Viewing Corridor*
(maquette)

Site & Sponsor: DRAC,
Ferme du Buisson, Noisiel F
Materials: Wood, Steel, Plexiglas,
Aluminum, Video Monitors
Dimensions: 33x22,5x210cm

Courtesy: Galerie des Archives,
Paris

A corridor is sited in the midst of
a Contemporary Arts Center
connecting the theatre space to
the cinema. Within are four video
monitors suspended along its
length displaying a video
program normally seen in the
interior cinema space of the
complex. The monitors are hung
sequentially in height forming a
positon reminiscent of a cinema
strip. Beneath are bleacher-like
seating, the kind used for temporary parades and
celebrations.
The viewer is placed in between
the suspended monitors and the
bench watching the image in
front while always being watched
from behind.

**62**

'The whole house with a roof, walls, windows and doors only lasts in fairy tales. Material and immaterial cables have penetrated it, have made Swiss cheese of it: antennae through the roof, telephone through the wall, television instead of windows and the car in a garage replacing the door.

The whole house became a ruin, through which blow the blizzards of communication. It calls for a new architecture, a new design.'

Vilém Flusser
*Vom Stand der Dinge*

Volgens Vilém Flusser doorboren hun coördinaten de architectuur. Nieuwe media ondermijnen de fysieke werkelijkheid, in plaats van deze te interpreteren.

De revolutionaire technologische ontwikkeling van de informatiemedia dwingt alle kaarten, alle symbolische orden en referentiële systemen zich in Real Time aan te passen aan veranderingen in het terrein dat ze weergeven. Aanwezigheid en tele-aanwezigheid, de gelijktijdige representatie van verschillende lokaties en het oplossen van geografische tijdzones in paralelle tijdspannen daagt kaartenmakers uit om de gebieden die ze in kaart willen brengen onafgebroken te surveilleren. Gevangen in onze informatieve zwerftochten zullen we tenminste evenveel, maar vrijwel zeker meer tijd op de kaart dan in het gebied doorbrengen. Informatiemedia zullen de werkelijkheid musealiseren, door hem van zijn vitale informatie te beroven, om met behulp daarvan een nieuwe werkelijkheid te vervaardigen, die de oude stuurt. Zo binden ze ons voorgoed in anonimiteit aan onze terminals.

Andrea Blum's recente werk, zoals *Surveillance Station(s)*, *Public Affairs* en *Information Plaza*, maar ook het nooit uitgevoerde *Video Viewing Corridor* en *Newsstand*, werd ontworpen om de onmiddellijke, lokale ervaring te verzoenen met informatie die buiten het gezichtsveld ligt maar in deze werken wordt geïmporteerd. Het jongste voorbeeld is *Information Plaza* (1996), dat op de campus van de TU Twente voorzichtig aanlegt aan het Internet en via electronische post tot on-line interactie uitnodigt (lichtkrant@utwente.nl). In het werk opgenomen lichtkranten brengen 24 uur per dag lokaal en internationaal nieuws. *Information Plaza* is letterlijk op zijn plaats omdat het bovenop het belangrijkste knooppunt van het glasvezelnet èn de nutsvoorzieningen is gebouwd. Het gebruik van landschappelijke elementen versterkt de materialiteit van het werk. Daarnaast is het echter volledig ontecht, dankzij de visuele overheersing van de immateriële externe informatie, die in de grote groene en rode LED lichtkranten wordt aangeboden.

Andrea Blum's onderzoek naar de informatisering van de openbaarheid sluit goed aan bij de intelligente culturele contextgevoeligheid die in sommige hedendaagse Nederlandse kunst voor de openbare ruimte wordt gelegd (zoals zich met name in de activiteiten van het Praktijkbureau voor Beeldende Kunstopdrachten van de

een subtiel en inzichtelijk evenwicht tussen de documentatie van Stroom, zijn representatie en jouw installatie—je kon je aandacht tussen deze zelfstandigheden verdelen, het brandpunt bewust verleggen. Maar de meubelwerken pakken je letterlijk in en bieden bescherming, tot je ontdekt dat je gedeeltelijk aan de blik van derden wordt blootgesteld.

**AB** De schaal van de meubelprojekten maakt ze een kruising tussen een object en een kleine kamer, waarmee ze het geheim van de aantrekkingskracht uitbuiten. Twee mensen zitten naast elkaar in een met vilt beklede bank; ze zien elkaars onderarm, verder niet, ze blijven anoniem. In al deze werken die een stukje nek laten zien, of een bovenbeen, een profiel of alleen een paar ogen, gebruik ik architectuur als vertelling.

En de context varieert. *Domestic Arrangement* was de titel van een serie galerietentoonstellingen in Parijs, Amsterdam en New York, waarin meubelprojekten als in een showroom werden gepresenteerd. Sommige zijn voor de privé-omgeving ontworpen, andere voor de semi-openbaarheid van een bankgebouw, wachtkamer, of lobby. Opgesteld in het museum zouden ze dienst kunnen doen om van daaruit naar andere kunst te kijken. Van mij mag het museum wat toegankelijker zijn en interactiever met zijn publiek omgaan: een soort ontheemd huis, een vluchtoord, een comfortabele plek. Ik hoop dat mijn werk

1988, *Newsstand #1 and #2*
(maquette)

Collaboration: Ken Kaplan/
Ted Krueger, architects

Materials: 'Honor Boxes',
Aluminum, Lexan,
LED Headline System, Telephone
Dimensions: 30x46x23cm

Sponsor: Public Art Fund, NYC

The *Newsstand* is pared down to
its basic function of
disseminating information.
The design development first
isolates the *Newsstand* operator
from the news, then eliminates
the operator altogether, thereby
becoming a totally automated
news station. It includes the addition of a telephone booth and
time/temperature as other important street concerns.
The selling of conventional
newspapers by means of the
'honor box' system co-exists with
the electronic display of
headlines as a means to link the
news with the traffic of the street.
The headlines are communicated
in English and a second
language, as are the newspapers
displayed, both responsive to the
cultural identity of the
neighborhood in which the
*Newsstand* is located.

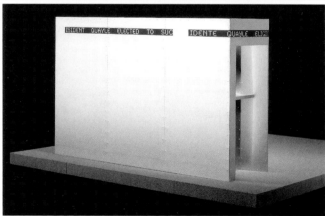

<twee mensen zitten naast elkaar in een met vilt beklede bank, ze zien elkaars onderarm

**64**

1991, *Urban Love Seat* (Bus Stop)
(maquette)

Materials: Aluminum,
Mirrored Glass
Dimensions: 180x60x90cm
(each module)

A curved modulated structure of
undetermined length is placed on
an urban street, establishing a
row of seating for individuals
waiting for a bus or just desiring
to sit down.
Each compartment is separated
from the other and made of
2-way mirror.The structure is
translucent and reflective.

ertoe bijdraagt dat de gebruiker zich op verschillende manieren opstelt, in verschillende omgevingen...

JK Waarom gebruik je daar zo'n ingehouden architektuur voor? Wil je vermijden dat de architecturale kwaliteiten van je werk de promiscuïteit van de interactie teveel aanmoedigen?

AB De terughoudendheid van de vorm versterkt de complexiteit van het 'kijkgat'.

JK Onze omgangsvormen raakten op drift tussen de privéomgeving en de openbaarheid. We zien een voortdurende verschuiving van de functies van onze omgevingen en van de instituties en regels die deze bepalen en inrichten. Komt er een dag waarop we voor een beetje privacy ons huis uit moeten? Wanneer onze eigen ruimtes zo met media en informatie gevuld zullen zijn dat ze onleefbaar worden? Als privacy alleen nog door anonimiteit wordt gegarandeerd en alleen onbekendheid, naamloosheid, ons privacy biedt? Laten we nog wel sporen achter als we de straten moeten doorkruisen, om met een boog om ons door mediaspoken belegerde huis heen te lopen?

1988, *Landfill* (Bus Station)

Collaboration: Dennis Adams

Site: West Street Battery Park City,
New York
Materials: Cast Concrete,
Aluminum, Lexan, Fluorescent
Lights, Duratrans
Dimensions: 1,2x7,6x2,4m

Sponsor: Olympia & York
Battery Park City

*Landfill* was designed for the exhibition 'The New Urban Landscape'. Battery Park City is built on landfill and, in addition to being a housing complex, is the new Financial Center of New York; the three towers leased to AT&T, Merrill Lynch and American Express.

Our approach was to design a functional bus station which would reference the traffic network of the site and its pedestrian walkways while simultaneously making inference to the investment holdings of the formerly mentioned companies in South Africa. The advertising vernacular of the 'sign' was displaced from its typical elevated location to one which sank into the the sidewalk, below eye level. The image, no longer of sales, but of a South African funeral procession. The coffin and its attendants compose a structural relationship with the bench slab and those waiting for the bus. The project posed questions about the intricacies of the flow of capital and the public's complicity with this arrangement.

<de terughoudendheid van de vorm versterkt de complexiteit van het 'kijkgat'

**66**

Mondriaan Stichting, dat de totstandkoming van de
*Plaza* mede mogelijk maakte, manifesteert). Een eerdere
installatie in de Nederlandse context, *Public Affairs*
(1995) voor Stroom hcbk, ontpopte zich als een verhulde
domesticatie van vijf jaar opdrachtenbeleid van deze
instelling. Het tentoonstellingsontwerp omvatte verschillende stukken modulair meubilair, een soort object-
kamers, die elk voor de presentatie van documentatie in
een ander medium waren toegerust. Projekten van colle-
ga-kunstenaars, die ook voor het merendeel anti-monumentaal waren, tijdelijk en vluchtig, werden hier geïnfor-
matiseerd en als dia, geluid, video, in druk of als publika-
tie gedistribueerd.

#### het huis: conclusie
In Andrea Blum's installaties en projekten zullen we
nooit in anonimiteit kunnen (be-)rusten. Haar werken
geven interactie een plaats. Ze sturen ons motorische
geheugen, griffen een herinnering in ons 'lichaam dat
niet vergeet' en stimuleren tegelijkertijd de vorming van
intelligente plattegronden en communicatiesystemen, die
de psychologische constructie van onze waarneming en de
politisering van onze identiteit blootleggen.

Terwijl haar werk in de openbare ruimte zich de laatste
jaren meer dan voorheen op informatie betrekt, die de
eenheid van ruimte en tijd veronachtzaamt, bouwt ze ook
aan *Domestic Arrangement*, waarin alle aandacht gericht
is op de directe ervaring van intimiteit, idiosyncrasie en
privacy. Andrea Blum brengt het uit gewoontehandelin-
gen opgetrokken huis van Berger, het in onze motoriek
gegrifte huis van Bachelard en het door medialisering
geruïneerde huis van Flusser op dezelfde kaart. In hun
anti-monumentaliteit zijn haar projekten werkelijk demo-
cratisch, inderdaad een thuis, een gewone en gemeen-
schappelijke open plek voor uitwisseling, waar informatie
vitaal is en aanwezigheid de voorwaarde.

AB Vijftien jaar geleden had de straat een andere functie dan tegenwoordig. Het was een arena om te flaneren, rond te hangen, elkaar voor seksuele avonturen op te pikken, het was amusement. Nu hebben we geen tijd meer om rond te hangen, AIDS heeft de balts in de straat achterhaald en daklozen hebben de plekken met een hoog amusementsgehalte in bezit genomen. Het leven op straat is vervlakt, mensen zijn er bang geworden, bang voor hun veiligheid, bang te laat te komen, angstig getuige te wor-den van een gebeurtenis die ze in gewetensnood brengt...

JK Je werken in de openbare ruimte zijn er op gericht de tred van het publiek te vertragen, het tot stilstand te brengen... je wilt ons tempo verlagen tot we erbij gaan zitten om ons te verbazen en de situatie te onderzoeken...?

AB Ik zie mijn werk als een filmstrook die vertraagd wordt afgedraaid, waarbij details worden uitvergroot en het eigenlijke ver-haal gaan vormen. Je ziet de regels gemaakt en overtreden worden, bewegingen worden ingezet en verschuiven...

JK Ook een ruimte of plek of installatie die zichzelf niet overduidelijk als kunst aanbeveelt zal als 'anders' herkend worden: als iets anders dan een faciliteit, iets anders dan een stuk straatmeubilair. Dit alarmeert de kijker en maakt sommigen gevoelig voor

1990, *Sunken Network System*

Site: Fillmore Center, Fillmore and
O'Farrell St. San Francisco CA
Materials: Cast Concrete, Water,
Light, Landscape Material
Dimensions: Plaza 120 sqm

Sponsor: Fillmore Center and
Redevelopment Corporation for
the City of San Francisco

The site is inscribed with two sets
of access routes, one being water
troughs, the other, walkways.
A third is marked by a number of
bench/slab structures which
designate private space within the
public space of access. The plaza
is layed out like a cartographic
system, notating the possibilities
for entrance and exit to and from
the outlining neighborhood.
The project becomes a 'life-line'
attempting to re-connect the
development complex to its
community.

<vijftien jaar geleden had de straat een andere functie dan tegenwoordig

**70**

1990, *Livonia*

Site: Civic Center, Livonia MI
Materials: Cast Concrete,
Steel Railing, Light
Dimensions: 3x18x18m

Sponsor: City of Livonia,
Michigan, National Endowment
for the Arts, Art in Public
Places Commission

A site is located within a Civic
Center of a Detroit suburb. It is
surrounded by a city hall and a
police station.
Within the site is a project
designed to mimic the structure
of the surrounding buildings in
look and function, though it has
been placed in an underground
location.
The project is now transformed
resembling a bunker. It is now
hidden from view and made
accessible for public use.

een ervaring. 'Kunst' doet dit. Jouw werk laat zich, ook als het niet zozeer als 'kunst' wordt aanbevolen, vrij gemakkelijk herkennen als iets met een andere functie of bedoeling en ʇrekt zo de aandacht. Loop je niet het risico vrijblijvend te worden? Er worden toch zekere regels door het werk opgelegd, die op een onopvallende manier de receptie sturen en de omgeving domineren? Je 'knelpunten' dwingen de blik van de gebruiker in een bepaalde richting en verlenen deze een bepaalde kwaliteit.

**AB** Elk werk stelt zijn eigen regels. *Sunken Network System* in San Francisco kent drie navigatiesystemen, die zo ontworpen zijn dat ze de plek opnieuw met de buurt waarin hij ligt integreren. In *Benches & Walkways* kreeg ik te maken met een padenstelsel op een campus waar de studenten zich niets van aantrokken: ze sneden alle officiële wegen af. Ik verhardde het nieuwe padenpatroon van de studenten, als een soort voorschot op het feit dat hun wensen de universitaire kaart telkens vernieuwen.

In de grootschalige werken in de openbaarheid krijgen architectonische knelpunten vorm in netwerken en doorgangen. In de meubelwerken vormen de blootgestelde lichaamsdelen een ongemakkelijkheid.

**JK** De vertraging waarin de 'tekst' en de 'subtekst' worden omgekeerd is een krachtig mechanisme dat door het werk wordt ver-

<in de meubelwerken vormen de blootgestelde lichaamsdelen een ongemakkelijkheid

**72**

1989, *Rotational Shift*

Site: Computer Science Building
Plaza at the University of
Wisconsin at Madison.
Materials: Cast Concrete,
Steel Railing, Lights,
Landscape Material.
Dimensions: 1,5x38x23m

Sponsor: Wisconsin State Arts
Commission and the
University of Wisconsin

Sited between the Computer
Science Building and the Student
Union, *Rotational Shift* is
designed to notate the pedestrian
traffic patterns moving between
the buildings and across the
street. This information is built
into the project, investing the site
with the history of its use.
Throughout, areas are
established to augment this
relationship, functioning as
markers for a range of social
interactions to occur.
The plaza is framed by two
multistoried buildings offering a
birdseye view of the activity
below. The view allows for a
cinematic reading of the site,
where public function is
combined with private
idiosyncracy.

sterkt. De schaal van de *interface* verandert met de ruimtelijke en psychologische omgeving van het werk, met de contextuele stemming, met de ruimtelijke stemmingen van materiaal, oppervlakte en licht, volume en afstand. Het zijn ruimtes die dicht zouden kunnen klappen, zoals je in beeld-voor-beeld filmanimatie ziet, *freeze frame*...

**AB** Er is een prachtige film van Kurasawa, 'DoDesKaDen', uit 1970. Op een gegeven moment zie je twee dronken kerels, die in een sloppenwijk van Tokyo wonen, de weg naar huis zoeken. De krotten zien er allemaal hetzelfde uit, behalve dat ze een soort kleurencode hebben. Elk van de twee mannen zoekt zich een weg naar huis door de kleur van zijn hoofdband te vergelijken met de kleur van de krotten, tot hij eindelijk de passende vindt. Onze stedelijke ruimte heeft bijna geen eigen visuele kenmerken meer. Huizencomplexen hebben buurten vervangen en luchthavens werden winkelcentra. Net als de mannen in Kurasawa's film zoeken we naar aanwijzingen die ons naar huis kunnen leiden.

**JK** We moeten de straat op om de weg naar huis te vinden—om onze 'hoofdbanden te vergelijken' en andere gewoonten aan te leren. Dat herinnert me aan John Berger. Hij schrijft dat we ons eerder thuis voelen in gewoontes dan in een huis. We kiezen de gewoontes zelf, ze worden niet opgelegd. Ons huis is niet langer een behuizing, maar een levensverhaal.

< we zoeken naar aanwijzingen die ons naar huis kunnen leiden

1989, *Street Link*

Site: Sunrise Park, Dayton OH
Materials: Cast Concrete,
Steel Railing, Earth
Dimensions: 2x48x22m

Sponsor: Dayton City Beautiful,
City of Dayton

A park runs along the Miami
River across from downtown
Dayton it functions as a border
between the city and a lower
income neighborhood of small
family housing units.

The project cuts into the
landscape of the park to serve as
a busstop as well as an overlook
towards the downtown area of
the city.
The gap between the City and the
neighborhood is illusionistically
removed by this gesture.

AB Onze huiselijke gewoontes worden op straat voortgezet. Ons lopen, praten, eten, ontspannen wordt op de schaal van de openbaarheid aangescherpt. Als we ons huis uitgaan slepen we het de hele dag mee alsof het een rugzak is. We nemen het mee de straat op, naar het theater, de ondergrondse in, naar het winkelcentrum. We dragen de muren, stoelen, boekenkast en onze spulletjes mee. Onze jas voelt als een warm bad. De krant past ons als een *mobile home*. In het park zitten we op hetzelfde bankje als gisteren. We drinken koffie om de openbare ruimte huiselijker te maken. In de trein verstoppen we ons in een boek. Onze zonnebril scheidt onze kamer van andere af. In de reflectie in autoruiten proberen we een glimp op te vangen van de context van onze aanwezigheid. We steken de straat over en vragen ons af waarom we ons huis verlieten.

New York 12-13 oktober 1995

< we drinken koffie om de openbare ruimte huiselijker te maken

1985, *Benches and Walkways*

Site: East Carolina University,
Greenville NC
Material: Cast Concrete
Dimensions: 0,47x1,52x48m

Sponsor: East Carolina University,
School of Art

Four walkways cross a college
campus. Their location follow the
ones trodden by the students in
disregard of the formalized
system built by the university.
These walkways are punctuated
by round benches located at
various points within the overall
system, establishing sites for
different social interactions to
occur. Superimposed on top of
this network is a schematic map
cast into the surface of the
concrete which visually connects
this site to the larger university
complex.

# The Story of the Fourth Wise Man

## Henry Van Dyke

Retold by Juliet Ellis-Behnke

# The Story of the Fourth Wise Man

By Henry van Dyke

Retold by Juliet Ellis-Behnke

ISBN 978-1623390211
Revised and annotated edition
Originally published under the title *The Story of the Other Wise Man*

*Plus the Ink*
An imprint at Minus the Ink Digital Publishing Group

# PREFACE

It is now several years since this little story was set
afloat on the sear of books. It is not a man of war, nor
even a high-sided merchantman; only a small, peaceful
sailing-vessel. Yet it has had rather an adventurous
voyage. Twice it has fallen into the hands of pirates.
The tides have carried it to far countries. It has been
passed through the translator's port of entry into Ger-
man, French, Armenian, Turkish, and perhaps some
other foreign regions. Once I caught sight of it flying
the outlandish flag of a brand-new phonetic language
along the coasts of France; and once it was claimed by
a dealer in antiquities as a long-lost legend of the Ori-
ent. Best of all, it has slipped quietly into many a fara-
way harbor that I have never seen, and found a kindly
welcome, and brought back messages of good cheer
from unknown friends.

Now it has turned home to be new-rigged and fitted
for further voyaging. Before it is sent out again I have
been asked to tell where the story came from and what
it means.

I do not know where it came from - out of the air,
perhaps. One thing is certain, it is not written in any
other book, nor is it to be found among the ancient love
of the East. And yet I have never felt as it were my
own. It was a gift. It was sent to me; and it seemed as if
I knew the Giver, though His name was not spoken.

The year had been full of sickness and sorrow. Every day brought trouble. Every night was tormented with
pain. They are very long - those nights when one lies

awake, and hears the laboring heart pumping wearily at its task, and watches for the morning, not knowing whether it will ever dawn. They are not nights of fear; for the thought of death grows strangely familiar when you have lived with it for a year. Besides, after a time you come to feel like a soldier who has been long standing still under fire; any change would be a relief. But they are lonely nights; they are very heavy nights. And their heaviest burden is this: You must face the thought that your work in the world may be almost ended, but you know that it is not nearly finished.

You have not solved the problem that perplexed you. You have not reached the goal that you aimed at. You have not accomplished the great task that you set for yourself. You are still on the way; and perhaps our journey must end now - nowhere - in the dark.

Well, it was in one of these long, lonely nights that this story came to me. I had studied and loved the curious tales of the Three Wise Men of the East as they are told in the "Golden Legend" of Jacobus de Voragine and other medieval books. But of the Fourth Wise Man I had never heard until that night. Then I saw him distinctly, moving through the shadows in a little circle of light. His countenance was as clear as the memory of my father's face as I saw it for the last time a few months before. The narrative of his journeyings and trials and disappointments ran without a break. Even certain sentences came to me complete and unforgettable, clear-cut like a cameo. All that I had to do was to follow Artaban, step by step, as the tale went on, from the beginning to the end of his pilgrimage.

Perhaps this map explains some things in the story. I have been asked many times why I made the Fourth Wise Man tell a lie, in the cottage at Bethlehem, to save the little child's life.

I did not make him tell a lie.

What Artaban said to the soldiers he said for himself, because he could not help it.

Is a lie ever justifiable? Perhaps not. But may it not sometimes seem inevitable?

And if it were a sin, might not a man confess it, and be pardoned for it more easily than for the greater sin of spiritual selfishness, or indifference, or the betrayal of innocent blood? That is what I saw Artaban do. That is what I heard him say. All through his life he was trying to do the best that he could. It was not perfect. But there are some kinds of failure that are better than success.

Though the story of the Fourth Wise Man came to me suddenly and without labor, there was a great deal of study and toil to be done before it could be written down. An idea arrives without effort; a form can only be wrought out by patient labor. If your story is worth telling, you ought to love it enough to be willing to work over it until it is true, true not only to the ideal, but true also to the real. The light is a gift; but the local color can only be seen by one who looks for it long steadily. Artaban went with me while I toiled through a score of volumes of ancient history and travel. I saw his figure while I journeyed on the motionless sea of the desert and in the strange cities of the East.

And now that his story is told, what does it mean?

How can I tell? What does life mean? If the meaning could be put into a sentence there would be no need of telling the story.

Henry van Dyke

# THE STORY OF THE FOURTH WISE MAN

# TABLE OF CONTENTS

# THE SIGN IN THE SKY

# CHAPTER I
# THE SIGN IN THE SKY

In the days when Augustus Caesar was master of many kings and Herod reigned in Jerusalem, a man named Artaban lived in the city of Ecbatana, among the mountains of Persia. His house was close to the outermost of the walls which formed a circle around the royal treasury. From his roof he could look over the seven parapets of black, white, crimson, blue, red, silver and gold to the hill where the summer palace of the Parthian emperors glittered like a jewel in a crown.

Surrounding Artaban's house was a beautiful garden: a tangle of flowers and fruit-trees, watered by a score of streams descending from the slopes of Mount Orontes, with music from innumerable birds. But on this late September night all color was lost in the soft and odorous darkness, and all sounds were hushed in the deep charm of its silence, except for water splashing, like a voice half-sobbing and half-laughing under the shadows. High above the trees a dim glow of light shone through the curtained arches of the great room, where Artaban had gathered together his friends for a meeting.

He stood by the doorway to greet his guests. He was a tall, dark man about forty, with brilliant eyes set close together under his broad brow, and firm lines that formed a groove around his fine, thin lips. He had the brow of a dreamer and the mouth of a soldier; a man of sensitive feeling, but inflexible will--one of those who,

1

in whatever age they may live, are born for inward conflict and a life of quest.

He wore a robe of pure white wool, thrown over a tunic of silk; his white, pointed cap, with long lapels at the sides, rested on his flowing black hair. It was the dress of the ancient priesthood of the Magi, called the fire-worshippers.

"Welcome!" he said, in his low, pleasant voice, as one after another entered the room. "Welcome, Abdus; peace be with you, Rhodaspes and Tigranes, and with you my father, Abgarus. You are all welcome. This house grows brighter with the joy of your presence."

There were nine men, differing widely in age, but alike in the richness of their dress of many-colored silks and in the massive golden collars around their necks, marking them as Parthian nobles; and in the winged circles of gold resting upon their breasts, the sign of the followers of Zoroaster.

They took their places around a small black altar at the end of the room, where a tiny flame was burning. Artaban, standing beside it, waved a bundle of thin tamarisk branches above the fire, feeding it with dry sticks of pine and fragrant oils. Then he began the ancient chant of the Yasna, and the voices of his companions joined in the hymn to Ahura-Mazda:

*We worship the Spirit Divine,*
*all wisdom and goodness possessing,*
*Surrounded by Holy Immortals,*
*the givers of bounty and blessing;*
*We joy in the work of His hands,*
*His truth and His power confessing.*

*We praise all the things that are pure,*
*        for these are His only Creation*
*The thoughts that are true, and the words*
*        and the deeds that have won approbation;*
*These are supported by Him,*
*        and for these we make adoration.*
*Hear us, O Mazda! Thou livest*
*        in truth and in heavenly gladness;*
*Cleanse us from falsehood, and keep us*
*        from evil and bondage to badness,*
*Pour out the light and the joy of Thy life*
*        on our darkness and sadness.*

*Shine on our gardens and fields,*
*        shine on our working and waving;*
*Shine on the whole race of man,*
*        believing and  unbelieving;*
*Shine on us now through the night,*
*Shine on us now in Thy might,*
*The flame of our holy love*
*        and the song of our worship receiving.*

The fire rose with the chant, throbbing as if the flame responded to the music, until it illuminated the whole apartment, revealing its simplicity and splendor.

The floor was laid with tiles of dark blue veined with white; pilasters of twisted silver stood out against the blue walls; the clerestory of round-arched windows above them was hung with azure silk; the vaulted ceiling was a pavement of blue stones, like the body of heaven in its clearness, sown with silver stars. From the four corners of the roof hung four golden magic-wheels, called the tongues of the gods. At the eastern end, behind the altar, there were two dark-red pillars of stone; above them a lintel of the same, on which was carved the figure of a winged archer, with his arrow set to the string and his bow drawn.

The doorway between the pillars, which opened on the terrace of the roof, was covered with a heavy curtain the color of a ripe pomegranate, embroidered with innumerable golden rays shooting upward from the floor. In effect the room was like a quiet, starry night, all azure and silver, flushed in the cast of the rosy promise of dawn. It was, as the house of a man should be, an expression of the character and spirit of the master.

He turned to his friends when the song ended, and invited them to sit on the chairs at the western end of the room.

"You have come tonight," he said, looking around the circle, "at my call, as the faithful scholars of Zoroaster, to renew your worship and rekindle your faith in the God of Purity, even as this fire has been rekindled on the altar. We do not worship the fire, but Him of whom it is the chosen symbol, because it is the purest of all created things. It speaks to us of one who is Light and Truth. Isn't it so, my father?"

"It is well said, my son," answered the venerable Abgarus. "The enlightened never worship idols. They lift the veil of form and go into the shrine of reality, and new light and truth come to them continually through the old symbols." "Hear me, then, my father and my friends," said Artaban, "while I tell you of the new light and truth that have come to me through the most an-

4

cient of all signs. We have searched the secrets of Nature together, and studied the healing virtues of water and fire and the plants. We have also read the books of prophecy in which the future is dimly foretold in words that are hard to understand. But the highest of all learning is the knowledge of the stars. To trace their course is to untangle the threads of the mystery of life from the beginning to the end. If we could follow them perfectly, nothing would be hidden from us. But our knowledge of them is still incomplete, There are many stars still beyond our horizon--lights that are known only to the dwellers in the far south lands, among the spice trees of Punt and the gold mines of Ophir."

There was a murmur of assent among the listeners.

"The stars," said Tigranes, "are the thoughts of the Eternal. They are numberless. But the thoughts of man can be counted, like the years of his life. The wisdom of the Magi is the greatest of all wisdoms on earth, because it knows its own ignorance. And that is the secret of power. We keep men always looking and waiting for a new sunrise. But we ourselves understand that the darkness is equal to the light, and that the conflict between them will never be ended."

"That doesn't satisfy me," answered Artaban, "for, if the waiting is endless, if there is no fulfilment of it, then it wouldn't be wise to look and wait. We should become like those new teachers of the Greeks, who say that there is no truth, and that the only wise men are those who spend their lives in discovering and exposing the lies that have been believed in the world. But the new sunrise will certainly appear in the appointed time.

Don't our own books tell us that this will come to pass, and that men will see the brightness of a great light?"

"That's true," said the voice of Abgarus, "every faithful disciple of Zoroaster knows the prophecy of the Avesta, and carries the word in his heart. `In that day Sosiosh the Victorious will arise out of the number of the prophets in the east country. Around him will shine a mighty brightness, and he will make life everlasting, incorruptible and immortal; and the dead shall rise again.' "

"This is a dark saying," said Tigranes, "and it may be that we will never understand it. It's better to consider the things that are near at hand, and to increase the influence of the Magi in their own country, rather than to look for one who may be a stranger, and to whom we must resign our power."

The others seemed to approve these words. There was a silent feeling of agreement among them; their looks responded with that indefinable expression which always follows when a speaker has uttered the thought that has been slumbering in the hearts of his listeners. But Artaban turned to Abgarus with a glow on his face, and said: "My father, I have kept this prophecy in the secret place of my soul. Religion without a great hope would be like an altar without a living fire. And now the flame has burned more brightly, and by the light of it I have read other words which have also come from the fountain of Truth, and speak yet more clearly of the rising of the Victorious One in his brightness."

He drew from the breast pocket of his tunic two small rolls of fine parchment, with writing on them, and unfolded them carefully upon his knee.

6

"In the years that are lost in the past, long before our fathers came into the land of Babylon, there were wise men in Chaldea, from whom the first of the Magi learned the secret of the heavens. And of these Balaam, the son of Beor, was one of the mightiest. Hear the words of his prophecy: 'There will come a star out of Jacob, and a new authority will arise out of Israel.' "

The lips of Tigranes drew downward with contempt, as he said: "Judah was a captive by the waters of Babylon, and the sons of Jacob were in bondage to our kings. The tribes of Israel are scattered through the mountains like lost sheep, and from the remnant that dwells in Judea under the yoke of Rome, neither star nor authority will arise."

"And yet," answered Artaban, "it was the Hebrew Daniel, the mighty searcher of dreams, the counselor of kings, the wise Belteshazzar, who was most honored and beloved of our great King Cyrus. A prophet of sure things and a reader of the thoughts of the Eternal, Daniel proved himself to our people, and he wrote (Artabus read from the second scroll): " 'Know, therefore, and understand that from the going forth of the commandment to restore Jerusalem, unto the Anointed One, the Prince, the time shall be sixty-seven and two weeks. ' "

"But, my son," said Abgarus, doubtfully, "these are mystical numbers. Who can interpret them or find the key that shall unlock their meaning?"

Artaban answered: "It has been shown to me and to my three companions among the Magi--Caspar, Melchior, and Balthazar. We have searched the ancient tablets of Chaldea and computed the time. It falls in this year. We have studied the sky, and in the spring of the year we saw two of the greatest planets draw near together in the sign of the Fish, which is the house of the Hebrews. We also saw a new star there, which shone for one night and then vanished. Now, again, the two great planets are meeting. Tonight is their conjunction. My three brothers are watching by the ancient Temple of the Seven Spheres, at Borsippa in Babylonia, and I am watching here. If the star shines again, they'll wait ten days for me at the temple, and then we'll leave together for Jerusalem, to see and worship the promised one who will be born King of Israel. I believe the sign will come. I'm ready for the journey. I sold all of my possessions and bought these three jewels--a sapphire, a ruby, and a pearl--to carry them as tribute to the King. And I'm asking you to go with me on the pilgrimage that we may have joy together in finding the Prince who is worthy to be served."

While he was speaking he thrust his hand into the innermost fold of his tunic and drew out three great gems--one blue as a fragment of the night sky, one redder than a ray of sunrise, and one as pure as the peak of a snow-mountain at twilight--and laid them on the outspread scrolls before him.

But his friends looked at him with strange and alien eyes. A veil of doubt and mistrust came over their faces, like a fog creeping up from the marshes to hide the hills. They glanced at each other with looks of wonder and pity, as those who have listened to incredible sayings, the story of a wild vision, or the proposal of an impossible enterprise.

At last Tigranes said: "Artaban, this is a vain dream. It comes from looking at the stars too much and cherishing lofty thoughts. It would be wiser to spend the time gathering money for the new fire-temple at Chala. No king will ever rise from the broken race of Israel, and no end will ever come to the eternal strife of light and darkness. He who looks for it is a chaser of shadows. Farewell."

And another said: "Artaban, I have no knowledge of these things, and my office as guardian of the royal treasure binds me here. The quest is not for me. But if you must follow it, I wish you well."

And another said: "I have a new bride, and I cannot leave her nor take her with me on this strange journey. This quest is not for me. But may your steps be successful wherever you go. So, farewell."

So, one by one, they left Artaban's house. But Abgarus, the oldest and the one who loved him the best, lingered after the others had gone, and said, gravely: "My son, it may be that the light of truth is in this sign that has appeared in the skies, and then it will surely lead to the Prince and the mighty brightness. Or it may be that it's only a shadow of the light, as Tigranes said, and then he who follows it will have a long pilgrimage and a fruitless search. But it is better to follow even the shadow of the best than to remain content with the worst. And those who would see wonderful things must often be ready to travel alone. I am too old for this journey, but my heart will be a companion of your pilgrimage day and night, and I will know the end of your quest. Go in peace."

Then Abgarus went out of the azure chamber with its silver stars, and Artaban was left in solitude.

He gathered up the jewels and replaced them in his tunic. For a long time he stood and watched the flame that flickered and sank upon the altar. Then he crossed the hall, lifted the heavy curtain, and walked between the pillars of red stone to the terrace on the roof.

The shiver that runs through the earth as she rouses from her night-sleep had already begun, and the cool wind that heralds daybreak was drawing downward from the lofty snow-traced ravines of Mount Orontes. Birds, half-awakened, crept and chirped among the rustling leaves, and the smell of ripened grapes came in brief wafts from the arbors.

As Artaban watched them, a steel-blue spark sprang out of the darkness beneath, rounding itself with purple splendors to a crimson sphere, and shooting upward through rays of saffron and orange into a point of white radiance. Tiny and infinitely remote, yet perfect in every part, it pulsated in the enormous vault as if the three jewels in the Magian's tunic had mingled and been transformed into a living heart of light.

He bowed his head. He covered his brow with his hands. It is the sign," he said. "The King is coming, and I will go to meet him."

# BY THE WATERS OF BABYLON

# CHAPTER II
# BY THE WONDERS OF BABYLON

All night long, Vasda, the swiftest of Artaban's horses, had been waiting, saddled and bridled in her stall, pawing the ground impatiently and shaking her bit as if she shared the eagerness of her master's purpose.

Before the birds had fully roused to their strong, high, joyful chant of morning song, before the white mist had begun to lift lazily from the plain, the Fourth Wise Man was in the saddle, riding swiftly along the high road, which skirted the base of Mount Orontes, westward.

How close, how intimate is the comradeship between a man and his favorite horse on a long journey. It is a silent, comprehensive friendship, an interchange of thoughts beyond the need for words.

They drink at the same wayside springs and sleep under the same guardian stars. They are conscious together of the subduing spell of nightfall and the quickening joy of daybreak. The master shares his evening meal with his hungry companion and feels the soft mouth on the palm of his hand as it nibbles a morsel of bread. In the gray dawn he is awoken from his encampment by the gentle stir of warm breath over his sleeping face, and looks up into the eyes of his faithful fellow-traveler, ready and waiting for the toil of the day. Surely, unless he is a pagan and an unbeliever, by whatever name he calls his God, he will thank Him for this voiceless sympathy, this dumb affection, and his morning prayer will embrace a double blessing--God bless us both, the horse and the rider, and keep our feet from falling and our souls from death!

Then, through the crisp morning air, the swift hooves beat their tattoo along the road, keeping time to the pulsing of two hearts that move with the same eager desire--to conquer space, to devour the distance, to attain the goal of the journey.

Artaban had to ride wisely and well if he was to keep the appointed hour with the other Magi; for the route was five hundred miles, and fifty was the most that he could travel in a day. But he knew Vasda's strength and pushed forward without anxiety, making the fixed distance every day, though he had to travel late into the night, and in the morning long before sunrise.

He passed along the brown slopes of Mount Orontes, furrowed by the rocky courses of a hundred torrents.

He crossed the level plains of the Nisaeans, where the famous herds of horses, feeding in the wide pastures, tossed their heads at Vasda's approach and galloped away with a thunder of many hooves; and flocks of wild birds rose suddenly from the swampy meadows, wheeling in great circles with a shining flutter of innumerable wings and shrill cries of surprise.

He traversed the fertile fields of Concabar, where the dust from the threshing-floors filled the air with a golden mist, half hiding the huge temple of Astarte with its four hundred pillars.

At Baghistan, among the rich gardens watered by fountains from the rock, he looked up at the mountain thrusting its immense rugged brow out over the road and saw the figure of King Darius trampling upon his fallen foes, and the proud list of his wars and conquests engraved high upon the face of the eternal cliff.

Over many a cold and desolate pass, crawling painfully across the wind-swept shoulders of the hills; down black mountain-gorges, where the river roared and raced before him like a savage guide; across smiling vales, with terraces of yellow limestone full of vines and fruit-trees; through the oak-groves of Carine and the dark Gates of Zagros, walled in by precipices; into the ancient city of Chala, where the people of Samaria had been kept in captivity long ago; and out again by the mighty portal, riven through the encircling hills, where he saw the image of the High Priest of the Magi sculptured on the wall of rock, with hand uplifted as if to bless the centuries of pilgrims; past the entrance of the narrow defile, filled from end to end with orchards of peaches and figs, through which the river Gyndes foamed down to meet him; over the broad rice-fields, where the autumnal vapors spread their deathly mists; following along the course of the river, under tremulous shadows of poplar and tamarind, among the lower hills; and out upon the flat plain, where the road ran straight as an arrow through the stubble-fields and parched meadows; past the city of Ctesiphon, where the Parthian emperors reigned, and the vast metropolis of Seleucia which Alexander built; across the swirling floods of the Tigris and the many channels of the Euphrates, flowing yellow through the corn-lands. Artaban pressed onward until he arrived at nightfall on the tenth day, beneath the shattered walls of populous Babylon.

Vasda was nearly exhausted and Artaban would gladly have turned into the city to find rest and refreshment for himself and for her. But he knew that it was another three hours' journey to the Temple of the Seven Spheres, and he had to reach the place by midnight if he hoped to find his friends waiting. So he didn't stop, but rode steadily across the stubble-fields.

A grove of date-palms made an island of gloom in the pale yellow sea. As she passed into the shadow Vasda slowed her pace and began to pick her way more carefully.

Near the farther end of the darkness caution seemed to fall upon her. She sensed some danger or difficulty; it was not in her heart to run from it--only to be prepared for it and to meet it wisely, as a good horse should do. The grove was close and silent as a tomb; not a leaf rustled, not a bird sang.

She felt her steps before her delicately, carrying her head low and sighing now and then with apprehension. At last, she gave a quick breath of anxiety and dismay and stood stock-still, quivering in every muscle in front of a dark object in the shadow of the last palm-tree.

Artaban dismounted. The dim starlight revealed the form of a man lying across the road. His humble dress and the outline of his haggard face showed that he was probably one of the Hebrews who still lived in great numbers around the city. His pallid skin, dry and yellow as parchment, bore the mark of the deadly fever which ravaged the marsh-lands in autumn. The chill of death was in his lean hand and, as Artaban released it, the arm fell back inertly upon the motionless breast.

He turned away with a thought of pity, leaving the body to that strange burial which the Magians deemed most fitting: the funeral of the desert, from which the kites and vultures rise on dark wings and the beasts of prey slink furtively away. When they are gone there is only a heap of white bones on the sand.

But, as he turned, a long, faint, ghostly sigh came from the man's lips. The bony fingers gripped the hem of the Magian's robe and held him fast.

Artaban's heart leaped to his throat, not with fear, but with a dumb resentment at the importunity of this blind delay.

How could he stay here in the darkness to minister to a dying stranger? What claim had this unknown fragment of human life upon his compassion, or his service? If he lingered but for an hour he could hardly reach Borsippa at the appointed time. His companions would think he had given up the journey. They would go without him. He would lose his quest.

But if he went on now, the man would surely die. If Artaban stayed, life might be restored. His spirit throbbed and fluttered with the urgency of the crisis. Should he risk the great reward of his faith for the sake of a single deed of charity? Should he turn aside, if only for a moment, from the following of the star, to give a cup of cold water to a poor, perishing Hebrew?

"God of truth and purity," he prayed, "direct me in the holy path, the way of wisdom which only you know."

Then he turned back to the sick man. Loosening the grasp of his hand, he carried him to a little mound at the foot of the palm-tree.

He unbound the thick folds of the turban and opened the garment above the sunken breast. He brought water from one of the small canals nearby and moistened the sufferer's brow and mouth. He swirled a draught of one of those simple but potent remedies which he always carried in his tunic--for the Magians were physicians as well as astrologers--and poured it slowly between the colorless lips. Hour after hour he labored as only a skillful healer of disease can do. At last, the man's strength returned and he sat up and looked around.

"Who are you?" he said, in the rude dialect of the country, "and why have you sought me here to bring back my life?"

"I am Artaban the Magian, of the city of Ecbatana, and I am traveling to Jerusalem in search of one who is to be born King of the Jews, a great Prince and Deliverer of all men. I dare not delay any longer upon my journey, for the caravan that has waited for me may depart without me. But see, here is all that I have left of bread and wine and here is a potion of healing herbs. When your strength is restored you can find the dwellings of the Hebrews among the houses of Babylon."

The Jew raised his trembling hand solemnly to heaven.

"Now may the God of Abraham, Isaac and Jacob bless and prosper the journey of the merciful and bring him in peace to his desired haven. I have nothing to give you in return but this: that I can tell you where you must look for the Messiah, for our prophets have said that he will be born not in Jerusalem, but in Bethlehem.

May the Lord bring you in safety to that place, because you have had pity upon the sick."

It was already long past midnight. Artaban rode in haste and Vasda, restored by the brief rest, ran eagerly through the silent plain and swam the channels of the river. She regained her strength and fled over the ground like a gazelle.

But the first beam of the rising sun sent a long shadow before her as she reached the final stadium of the journey and the eyes of Artaban, anxiously scanning the great mound of Nimrod and the Temple of the Seven Spheres, could discern no trace of his friends.

The many-colored terraces of black, orange, red, yellow, green, blue and white, shattered by the convulsions of nature and crumbling under the repeated blows of human violence, still glittered like a ruined rainbow in the morning light.

Artaban rode swiftly around the hill. He dismounted and climbed to the highest terrace, looking out toward the west.

The huge desolation of the marshes stretched toward the horizon and the border of the desert. Herons stood by the stagnant pools and jackals skulked through the low bushes; but there was no sign of the caravan of the Wise Men, far or near.

At the edge of the terrace he saw a little heap of broken bricks; under them was a piece of papyrus. He caught it up and read: "We waited past midnight, and can delay no longer. We left to find the King. Follow us across the desert."

Artaban sat down upon the ground and covered his head in despair.

"How can I cross the desert," said he, "with no food and an exhausted horse? I must return to Babylon, sell my sapphire buy a train of camels, and provisions for the journey. I may never reach my friends. Only God the merciful knows whether I will miss seeing the King because I stopped to show mercy."

# FOR THE SAKE OF A LITTLE CHILD

# CHAPTER III
## FOR THE SAKE OF A LITTLE CHILD

There was a silence in the Hall of Dreams, where I was listening to the story of the Fourth Wise Man. Through this silence I saw, but very dimly, his figure passing over the dreary undulations of the desert, high upon the back of his camel, rocking steadily onward like a ship over the waves.

The land of death spread its cruel net around him. The stony waste bore no fruit but briers and thorns. The dark ledges of rock thrust themselves above the surface here and there, like the bones of perished monsters. Arid and inhospitable mountain ranges rose before him, furrowed with dry channels of ancient torrents, white and ghastly as scars on the face of nature. Shifting hills of treacherous sand were heaped like tombs along the horizon. By day, the fierce heat pressed its intolerable burden on the quivering air. No living creature moved on the swooning earth, except for tiny mice scuttling through the parched bushes, or lizards vanishing in the clefts of the rock. By night the jackals prowled and barked in the distance and the lion made the black ravines echo with his hollow roaring, while a bitter, blighting chill followed the fever of the day. Through heat and cold, the Magian moved steadily onward.

Then I saw the gardens and orchards of Damascus, watered by the streams of Abana and Pharpar, with their sloping swards inlaid with bloom, and their thickets of myrrh and roses. I saw the long, snowy ridge of Hermon, the dark groves of cedars, the valley of the Jordan, the blue waters of the Lake of Galilee, the fertile plain of Esdraelon, the hills of Ephraim and the highlands of Judah. Through all of these I followed the figure of Artaban moving steadily onward, until he arrived at Bethlehem. And it was the third day after the three Wise Men had come to that place and had found Mary and Joseph, with the young child, Jesus, and had laid their gifts of gold and frankincense and myrrh at his feet.

Then the Fourth Wise Man drew near, weary, but full of hope, bearing his ruby and his pearl to offer to the King. "For now at last," he said, "I surely shall find him, though I am alone and later than my brethren. This is the place where the Hebrew exile told me that the prophets had spoken, and here I shall see the rising of the great light. But I must ask about the visit of my brethren, and learn where the star directed them, and to whom they presented their tribute."

The streets of the village seemed to be deserted, and Artaban wondered whether the men had all gone up to the hill-pastures to bring down their sheep. From the open door of a cottage he heard the sound of a woman's voice singing softly. He entered and found a young mother hushing her baby to rest. She told him of the strangers from the Far East who had appeared in the village three days ago, and how they said that a star had guided them to the place where Joseph of Nazareth was lodging with his wife and her newborn child, and how they had paid reverence to the child and given him many rich gifts.

"But the travelers disappeared again," she continued, "as suddenly as they had come. We were afraid at the strangeness of their visit. We couldn't understand it.

The man of Nazareth took the child and his mother and fled away that same night secretly, and people whispered that they were going to Egypt. Ever since then there has been a sort of spell over the village; like something evil hangs over it. They say that the Roman soldiers are coming from Jerusalem to force a new tax from us and the men have driven the flocks and herds far back among the hills, and hidden themselves to escape it."

Artaban listened to her gentle, timid speech, and the child in her arms looked up in his face and smiled, stretching out its rosy hands to grasp at the winged circle of gold on his breast. His heart warmed to the touch. It seemed like a greeting of love and trust to one who had journeyed long in loneliness and perplexity, fighting with his own doubts and fears, and following a light that was veiled in clouds.

"Why couldn't this child have been the promised Prince?" he asked within himself, as he touched its soft cheek. "Kings have been born before now in lowlier houses than this, and the favorite of the stars may rise even from a cottage. But it seems that the God of wisdom is not rewarding my search so soon and so easily. The one whom I seek has gone before me; and now I must follow the King to Egypt."

The young mother laid the baby in its cradle and rose to attend to the wants of the strange guest that fate had brought into her house. She set food in front of him, the plain fare of peasants, but willingly offered and therefore full of refreshment for the soul as well as for the body. Artaban accepted it gratefully; and as he

25

ate, the child fell into a happy sleep, murmuring sweetly in its dreams. A great peace filled the room.

Suddenly there was a wild confusion in the streets of the village, women's voices shrieking and wailing, a clangor of brazen trumpets and a clashing of swords and a desperate cry: "The soldiers! The soldiers of Herod! They are killing our children."

The young mother's face grew white with terror. She held her child tightly and crouched motionlessly in the darkest corner of the room, covering him with the folds of her robe, lest he should wake and cry.

But Artaban went quickly and stood in the doorway of the house. His broad shoulders filled the portal from side to side and the peak of his white cap all but touched the lintel.

The soldiers came running down the street with bloody hands and dripping swords. At the sight of the stranger in his imposing dress they hesitated with surprise. The captain of the band approached the threshold to thrust him aside. But Artaban did not stir. His face was as calm as though he were watching the stars, and his eyes burned with that steady radiance that makes even the half-tamed hunting leopard shrink and the bloodhound pause in his leap. He held the soldier silently for an instant, and then said in a low voice: "I'm all alone in this place and I'm waiting to give this jewel to the prudent captain who will leave me in peace."

He showed the ruby, glistening in the hollow of his hand like a great drop of blood.

The captain was amazed at the splendor of the gem. The pupils of his eyes expanded with desire and the hard lines of greed wrinkled around his lips. He stretched out his hand and took the ruby.

"March on!" he cried to his men, "There is no child here. The house is empty."

The clamor and the clang of arms passed down the street as the headlong fury of the chase swept by the secret covert where the trembling woman was hidden. Artaban re-entered the cottage. He turned his face to the east and prayed: "God of truth, forgive my sin! I've told a lie, to save the life of a child. And two of my gifts are gone. I've spent for man that which was meant for God. Shall I ever be worthy to see the face of the King?"

But the voice of the woman, weeping for joy in the shadow behind him, said very gently:

"Because you have saved the life of my little one, may the Lord bless you and keep you; may the Lord make His face to shine upon you and be gracious unto you; may the Lord lift up His countenance upon you and give you peace."

IN THE HIDDEN
WAY OF SORROW

# CHAPTER IV
## IN THE HIDDEN WAY OF SORROW

Again there was a silence in the Hall of Dreams, deeper and more mysterious than the first interval, and I understood that the years for Artaban were flowing very swiftly under the stillness; and I caught only a glimpse, here and there, of the river of his life shining through the mist that concealed its course.

I saw him moving among the throngs of men in crowded Egypt, looking everywhere for traces of the household that had come down from Bethlehem, and finding them under the spreading sycamore-trees of Heliopolis, and beneath the walls of the Roman fortress of New Babylon beside the Nile: traces so faint and dim that they vanished before him continually, as footprints on the wet river-sand glisten for a moment with moisture and then disappear.

I saw him again at the foot of the pyramids, which lifted their sharp points into the intense saffron glow of the sunset sky, changeless monuments of the perishable glory and the imperishable hope of man. He looked up into the face of the crouching Sphinx and vainly tried to read the meaning of the calm eyes and smiling mouth. Was it the mockery of all effort and all aspiration, as the Tigranes had said: the cruel jest of a riddle that has no answer, a search that never can succeed? Or was there a touch of pity and encouragement in that inscrutable smile: a promise that even the defeated should attain a victory, the disappointed should discover a prize, the ignorant should be made wise, the blind should see and the wandering should come into the haven at last?

I saw him again in an obscure house in Alexandria, taking counsel with a Hebrew rabbi. The venerable man, bending over the rolls of parchment on which the prophecies of Israel were written, read aloud the pathetic words which foretold the sufferings of the promised Messiah--the despised and rejected of men, the man of sorrows and acquainted with grief.

"And remember, my son," he said, fixing his eyes upon the face of Artaban, "the King whom you seek is not to be found in a palace, nor among the rich and powerful. If the light of the world and the glory of Israel had been appointed to come with the greatness of earthly splendor, it must have appeared long ago. For no son of Abraham will ever again rival the power which Joseph had in the palaces of Egypt; or the magnificence of Solomon throned between the lions in Jerusalem. But the light for which the world is waiting is a new light, the glory that shall rise out of patient and triumphant suffering. And the kingdom which is to be established forever is a new kingdom, the royalty of unconquerable love.

"I do not know how this shall come to pass, nor how the turbulent kings and peoples of earth shall be brought to acknowledge the Messiah and pay homage to him. But this I know. Those who seek him will do well to look among the poor and the lowly, the sorrowful and the oppressed."

So I saw the Fourth Wise Man again and again, traveling from place to place, and searching among the people of the dispersion, with whom the little family from Bethlehem might, perhaps, have found a refuge. He passed through countries desperate with famine where the poor were crying for bread. He lived in plague-stricken cities where the sick were languishing in the bitter companionship of helpless misery. He visited the oppressed and the afflicted in the gloom of subterranean prisons, and the crowded wretchedness of slave-markets, and the weary toil of galley-ships. In all this populous and intricate world of anguish, though he found none to worship, he found many to help. He fed the hungry, and clothed the naked, and healed the sick, and comforted the captive; and his years passed more swiftly than the weaver's shuttle that flashes back and forth through the loom while the web grows and the pattern is completed.

It seemed almost as if he had forgotten his quest. But once I saw him for a moment as he stood alone at sunrise, waiting at the gate of a Roman prison. He had taken from a secret resting-place in his tunic the pearl, the last of his jewels. As he looked at it, a mellower luster, a soft and iridescent light, full of shifting gleams of azure and rose, trembled upon its surface. It seemed to have absorbed some reflection of the lost sapphire and ruby. So the secret purpose of a noble life draws into itself the memories of past joy and past sorrow. All that has helped it, all that has hindered it, is transfused by a subtle magic into its very essence. It becomes more luminous and precious the longer it is carried close to the warmth of the beating heart.

Then, at last, while I was thinking of this pearl, and of its meaning, I heard the end of the story of the Fourth Wise Man.

# A PEARL OF GREAT PRICE

# CHAPTER V
## A PEARL OF GREAT PRICE

Thirty-three years of Artaban's life had passed away and he was still a pilgrim and a seeker after light. His hair, once darker than the cliffs of Zagros, was now white as the wintry snow that covered them. His eyes that once flashed like flames of fire, were dull as embers smoldering among the ashes.

Worn and weary and ready to die, but still looking for the King, he had come for the last time to Jerusalem. He'd often visited the holy city before, and had searched all its lanes and crowded bevels and black prisons without finding any trace of the family of Nazarenes who had fled from Bethlehem long ago. But now it seemed as if he had to make one more effort, and something whispered in his heart that, at last, he might succeed.

It was the season of the Passover. The city was thronged with strangers. The children of Israel, scattered in far lands, had returned to the Temple for the great feast, and there had been a confusion of languages in the narrow streets for many days.

But on this day the multitudes were visibly agitated. The sky was veiled with a portentous gloom. Currents of excitement seemed to flash through the crowd. A secret tide was sweeping them all one way. The clatter of sandals and the soft, thick sound of thousands of bare feet shuffling over the stones flowed unceasingly along the street that leads to the Damascus gate.

Artaban joined a group of people from his own country, Parthian Jews who had come to keep the Passover, and inquired about the cause of the tumult, and where they were going.

"We are going," they answered, "to the place called Golgotha, outside the city walls, where there is to be an execution. Haven't you heard what happened? Two famous robbers are to be crucified, and with them another, called Jesus of Nazareth, a man who has done many wonderful works among the people, so that they love him greatly. But the priests and elders have said that he must die, because he said he is the Son of God. And Pilate has sent him to the cross because he said that he was the `King of the Jews.'

How strangely these familiar words fell upon the tired heart of Artaban! They had led him for a lifetime over land and sea. And now they came to him mysteriously, like a message of despair. The King had arisen, but he had been denied and cast out. He was about to perish. Perhaps he was already dying. Could it be the same who had been born in Bethlehem thirty-three years ago, at whose birth the star had appeared in heaven, and of whose coming the prophets had spoken?

Artaban's heart beat unsteadily with that troubled, doubtful apprehension which is the excitement of old age. But he said to himself: "The ways of God are stranger than the thoughts of men, and it may be that I shall find the King, at last, in the hands of his enemies, and shall come in time to offer my pearl for his ransom before he dies."

So the old man followed the multitude with slow and painful steps toward the Damascus gate of the city.

Just beyond the entrance of the guardhouse a troop of Macedonian soldiers came down the street, dragging a young girl with a torn dress and disheveled hair. As the Magian paused to look at her with compassion, she suddenly broke from the hands of her tormentors, and threw herself at his feet, clasping him around the knees. She had seen his white cap and the winged circle on his breast.

"Have pity on me," she cried, "and save me, for the sake of the God of Purity! I am also a daughter of the true religion which is taught by the Magi. My father was a merchant of Parthia, but he is dead, and I have been seized for his debts to be sold as a slave. Save me from worse than death!"

Artaban trembled.

It was the old conflict in his soul, the same that had come to him in the palm-grove of Babylon and in the cottage at Bethlehem--the conflict between the expectation of faith and the impulse of love. Twice the gift which he had consecrated to the worship of religion had been drawn to the service of humanity. This was the third trial, the ultimate test, the final and irrevocable choice.

Was this his great opportunity, or his last temptation? He couldn't tell. Only one thing was clear in the darkness of his mind--it was inevitable. And doesn't the inevitable come from God?

Of only one thing his divided heart was sure--to rescue this helpless girl would be a true deed of love. And isn't love the light of the soul?

He took the pearl from his tunic. Never had it seemed so luminous, so radiant, so full of tender, living luster. He laid it in the hand of the slave.

"This is your ransom, daughter! It is the last of my treasures which I kept for the King."

While he spoke, the darkness of the sky deepened and shuddering tremors ran through the earth, heaving convulsively like the chest of one who struggles with mighty grief.

The walls of the houses rocked to and fro. Stones were loosened and crashed into the street. Dust clouds filled the air. The soldiers fled in terror, reeling like drunken men. But Artaban and the girl whom he had ransomed crouched helplessly beneath the wall of the Praetorium.

What did he have to fear? What did he have to hope? He'd given away the last remnant of his tribute for the King. He'd parted with the last hope of finding him. The quest was over, and it had failed. But, even in that thought, accepted and embraced, there was peace. It wasn't resignation. It wasn't submission. It was something more profound and searching. He knew that all was well, because he had done the best that he could from day to day. He'd been true to the light that had been given to him. He had looked for more. And if he hadn't found it, if a failure was all that came out of his life, there was no doubt that it was the best that was possible. He hadn't seen the revelation of "life everlasting, incorruptible and immortal." But he knew that even if he could live his earthly life over again, it could not be any way other than it had been.

One more lingering pulsation of the earthquake quivered through the ground. A heavy tile, shaken from the roof, fell and struck the old man on the temple. He lay breathless and pale, with his gray head resting on the young girl's shoulder, blood trickling from the wound. As she bent over him, fearing that he was dead, there was a voice through the twilight, very small and still, like music sounding from a distance, in which the notes are clear but the words are lost. The girl turned to see if someone had spoken from the window above them, but she saw no one.

Then the old man's lips began to move, as if in answer, and she heard him say in the Parthian tongue: "Not so, my Lord! When did I see you hungry and fed you? Or thirsty, and give you drink? When did I see you as a stranger and take you in? Or naked and clothe you? When did I see you sick or in prison and come to you? For thirty-three years I've looked for you; but I've never seen your face, nor ministered to you, my King."

He stopped, and the sweet voice came again. And again the maid heard it, very faint and far away. But now it seemed as though she understood the words: "Verily I say unto you, inasmuch as you have done it unto one of the least of these my brethren, you have done it unto me."

A calm radiance of wonder and joy lit the pale face of Artaban like the first ray of dawn on a snowy mountain-peak. A long breath of relief exhaled gently from his lips.

His journey was ended. His treasures were accepted. The Fourth Wise Man had found the King.

HE END

# ABOUT HENRY VAN DYKE

Henry van Dyke (1852-1933) was born in Germantown, Pennsylvania, in the United States. He graduated from Princeton University in 1873 and from Princeton Theological Seminary in 1877; and served as a professor of English literature at Princeton between 1899 and 1923. In 1908–09 Dr. van Dyke was an American lecturer at the University of Paris. By appointment of President Wilson, a friend and former classmate of van Dyke, he became Minister to the Netherlands and Luxembourg in 1913. He was elected to the American Academy of Arts and Letters and received many other honors. He chaired the committee that wrote the first Presbyterian printed liturgy, The Book of Common Worship of 1906. He also wrote the lyrics to the popular hymn, "Joyful, Joyful We Adore Thee" (1907), sung to the tune of Beethoven's "Ode to Joy". The following quote is attributed to van Dyke, "Time is too slow for those who wait, too swift for those who fear, too long for those who grieve, too short for those who rejoice, but for those who love – time is eternity."